GREAT DAYS AT WORK

Praise for *Great Days at Work*

"Here is a book that brings together all for the advice, experience, rules of thumb and theory about achieving success and happiness in today's complex world. From the very first chapter, I found myself drawn into the narrative that uses well thought through examples, backed up by relevant theory to explain how a positive approach to setting goals, making decisions and focusing on the important activities can lead to a fulfilling and successful working life."

Mandy Chessell, IBM Distinguished Engineer, Visiting Professor, Department of Computer Science, University of Sheffield

"It is exciting and refreshing to see a self-help book so well grounded in psychology, distilling the extensive research base, yet remaining easy to read, understand and use as a practical tool. The evidence presented supports the ideas discussed and helps the reader to understand why doing things differently, in the ways suggested, will work. This book focuses on developing individual well-being and success, but would be equally useful to team builders and managers aiming to develop successful and more robust teams."

Dr Felicity Baker, C. Psychol., Director, East Midlands Psychology

"Many of the most important findings from recent psychology research have huge implications for our working lives, but these are often ignored or misunderstood in the business world. This book does a brilliant job of extracting the best of these insights and presenting them in a clear an engaging way for a business audience. This isn't "fluffy" or simplistic positive thinking; it gets to the heart of what helps human beings be at their best and contribute most in the long term. This book is packed with practical, evidence-based actions that have the potential to not only transform our personal experiences of working life, but to also revolutionise the way we run our organisations"

Dr Mark Williamson, Director, Action for Happiness

GREAT DAYS AT WORK

HOW POSITIVE PSYCHOLOGY CAN TRANSFORM YOUR WORKING LIFE

SUZANNE HAZELTON

First published in Great Britain and the United States in 2013 by Kogan Page Limited

120 Pentonville Road	1518 Walnut Street	4737/23 Ansari Road
London N1 9JN	Suite 1100	Daryaganj
United Kingdom	Philadelphia PA 19102	New Delhi 110002
www.koganpage.com	USA	India

© Suzanne Hazelton, 2013

Great Days Framework by Ethan Baker Eatough

The right of Suzanne Hazelton to be identified as the author of this work has been asserted by her in accordance with the Copyright, Designs and Patents Act 1988.

ISBN   978 0 7494 6923 8
E-ISBN   978 0 7494 6924 5

British Library Cataloguing-in-Publication Data

A CIP record for this book is available from the British Library.

Library of Congress Cataloging-in-Publication Data

Hazelton, Suzanne.
  Great days at work : how positive psychology can transform your working life / Suzanne Hazelton.
    pages cm
  Includes bibliographical references and index.
  ISBN 978-0-7494-6923-8 – ISBN (invalid) 978-0-7494-6924-5 1. Employee motivation.
2. Positive psychology. 3. Employees–Attitudes. 4. Performance–Psychological
aspects. 5. Quality of work life–Psychological aspects. I. Title.
  HF5549.5.M63H395 2013
  158.7–dc23

                                                                2013014334

Typeset by Graphicraft Limited, Hong Kong
Print production managed by Jellyfish
Printed and bound by CPI Group (UK) Ltd, Croydon CR0 4YY

Contents

Preface

As long as you live, keep learning how to live.

Seneca

I've spent over twenty years in business, starting my career in a technical role, as project manager then a people manager. I then moved into a training role where I designed and delivered personal and leadership development training courses, before moving into executive coaching. Over the years I've developed my skills in a number of areas, including psychotherapy; in the process I realized that my real passion is working with people to enable them to thrive and succeed.

Personal and professional development is my passion, and I've been immersed in the topic for over twenty years now, most recently studying the relatively new science of positive psychology. I've found some of what's 'common knowledge' around positive psychology a little saccharine sweet, and occasionally inaccurate. Some of the books are a little too obscure for the business professional, which undermines some of the enormous value from the field. I became interested in bringing some of the useful nuggets from the field to a broader readership of business professionals so that you can understand the latest research; these are areas that have strong evidence for their effectiveness and are not based on wishful thinking. This book will demonstrate how it applies to you, whether when making choices, decision making or working with others effectively.

With my understanding of psychotherapy and my experience of working with a number of business leaders I identified with the distinctly different approaches to leadership described by Kofodimos (1990): a *balanced* approach; and a *driven* approach. He describes:

> *Two sets of forces contributing to in-balance in executives, the rewards of the job vs the unfulfilling nature of personal life and the joy of mastery vs the threat of intimacy.*

What do I mean by a *driven* approach? There seem to be a number of patterns of behaviour that *driven* people 'do' that perhaps in a different context would be deemed unhealthy. For example, constant checking of one's Blackberry or iPhone in business is 'fine', whereas constant washing of hands would be considered obsessive compulsive disorder (OCD). In one organization I worked with there was a culture of very long hours, and weekend work was expected. To some extent there was a bias towards 'workaholism'. Addiction in any other context would be recognized and typically treated.

My goal in writing this book is to describe a balanced approach to having *great days at work*. Many of us realize that working 'smarter' and not 'longer' is more effective. Figure 0.1, the Yerkes–Dodson Curve, shows that whilst we need a certain level of stress to perform at our best, there is a point at which more stress leads to a plateauing of effectiveness, and eventually a gradual decline and sadly, in some cases, stress-related illness.

FIGURE 0.1   The balanced vs driven approach

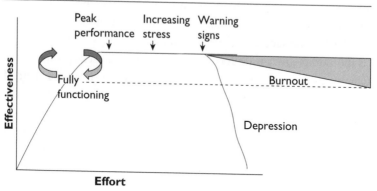

Adapted from the Yerkes–Dodson Curve

In athletes, peak performance is something that is strived for for a short period of time – prior to a significant race. Within business, how realistic is it to maintain 'peak performance'? We're effective at a point lower than 'peak', and interestingly and insidiously, burnout can be a slow process whereby people don't realize they're operating at less than peak.

Consider how effective you could be by operating at less than peak, knowing you can still shift to a higher level if the situation demands. At this level you can find time for networking, exercise, hobbies, interests and maintaining friendships, all of which are likely to increase your quality of life, your well-being and contribute to you having great days at work. Of course it's important that you're still effective in your job, and the research findings suggest that happier people are more successful on a range of measures – so improving your overall well-being will contribute to your success.

Research has shown that when we have purpose, mastery and autonomy we're likely to have intrinsic motivation – motivation that comes from within us. Mastery can be found in the workplace, as can purpose and autonomy.

This book is written for you the individual, no matter what your job title or role. Motivation isn't something that's done to another person (although a good manager or coach can unlock your motivation). This book will present you with some of the most important facts around the science of psychology so that you can make informed choices about what you can do for yourself.

Acknowledgements

Silent gratitude isn't much use to anyone.

G B Stern

The first thanks is to you, the reader, for taking the time to explore this book. Please take what's useful to you so that you can find new and different ways to have great days at work.

Over the years, I've been fortunate to have worked with so many inspirational colleagues and to have found mentors who have been influential in developing my thinking and emotions. The remainder of this section is a small piece of indulgence to formally thank some of these people: those who have inspired and those who have supported me through the writing and editing process to get this book published.

Ashley Bookman, CEO of Momentum; an inspirational thinker of our time. His team at Momentum have, over the years, also provided me with significant food for thought. Thanks to Doug Mofatt, Nigel Dennis, Ian Blair, Alex Hayward, Nick Dingley. I've had many awesome and inspirational colleagues within IBM – too many to list you all – but thank you. Those with whom I've worked and have been inspired by most recently include: Christine Lissoni, Alison Hoghton, Louis Larché and Mo Rye.

In my study of psychotherapy (Transactional Analysis), I've studied with and found both Adrienne Lee and Ian Stewart to be amazing trainers with a wealth of experience and knowledge.

In my studies of positive psychology I've been fortunate to study under Dr Boniwell, Dr Hefferon and Dr Popovic – they have incredible academic prowess, and have challenged my thinking and developed my academic rigour. My colleagues on the course have been a superb source of encouragement, positivity and inspiration.

Thank you too to all the people I've trained and coached – over the years there have been thousands of you – too many to name individually, but I've learned so much from you.

I'd like to also mention my 'friends' on Twitter for their frequent sparks of inspiration, intelligent blogs and links to current research.

I'd like to thank Pete Garrett for being a sounding board for matters requiring a military perspective – a perspective I'm not familiar with. I'd also like to thank his older brother Tim for being an awesome friend and supporter both during and since university.

A serendipitous chain of events put me in contact with Liz Gooster, Editor at Large with Kogan Page. I'd like to thank David Stewart and Matthew Flynn for facilitating the introduction, and a massive thanks to Liz for her edits, which have ensured a much stronger book with more business examples. I'd also like to thank Linda Dhondy for her edits and Nancy Wallace for her support, but any errors that remain are mine. Thanks to reviewers of early versions of this book, especially to Catherine Hawthorne and Louis Larché for their insightful comments.

I would like to give special thanks to Lucy Ryan for her assistance with clarifying the research in Chapter 11, and her significant contribution to the research section of that chapter.

Thanks to Ethan Baker Eatough for translating the Great Days Framework into something visually appealing.

Thanks to my many friends who've supported me in many ways through this process. Whilst some of my friends have read and commented on early versions, others have provided a glass of wine and encouragement or a good diversion. There are too many to list you all, but these deserve a special mention: Kathy Berry, Niki Buckingham, Sarah Brown, Darren Sayer, Lyn Hutchings, Sarah Ramsey, Debby Blamey, Shirley Smith, Angela Harkness, Majella Greene and Carole Stagg. You've been fabulous – thank you.

Thanks to my parents Colin and Ann Hazelton for their continued love, support and encouragement to do 'whatever makes you happy'; what better foundation from which to grow?

Finally thanks to my partner Angus Lyon for his continued support and encouragement, from his initial reading and editing of the early drafts of this book to making suggestions and being a FANTASTIC sounding board and endless source of encouragement. This 'behind the scenes' work is a pretty thankless task – but 'thank you'.

Introduction

A ship in a harbour is safe, that's not what ships were built for.

John A Shedd

Ahead of the curve

In today's highly competitive workforce, many of us are looking for an 'edge' – the difference that enables us to be successful. As unique beings we each define success in different ways; however, success is typically described in comparative terms, as in 'more successful than ...'. My personal belief is that we can each be successful – and the more successful we are as individuals, the more the institutions and communities around us, and that we're part of, will thrive.

Felicia Huppert (in Espen, 2006) suggests that the mental well-being of the population forms a standard distribution curve – with some people being exceptionally mentally healthy and others very dysfunctional, with a range of levels of well-being in between.

Often the target for government and mental health charities is increasing the mental functioning of the lowest in our society – however, Felicia argues for increasing well-being at higher stages as this will have a knock-on impact on society (Figure 0.2). I tend to agree; however, you don't have to subscribe to this view to read this book. *Great Days at Work* is about harnessing the latest scientific research for your benefit and your well-being.

FIGURE 0.2   The effect of shifting the mean of the mental health spectrum

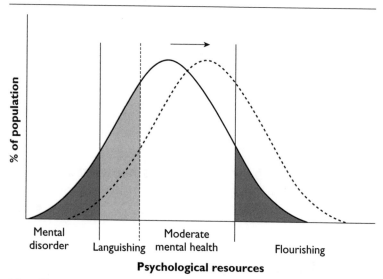

Adapted from Huppert (2009)

> At first I thought that the focus on an individual thriving seemed like it ignored some of the wider problems in society, until I remembered that communities and organizations are comprised of individuals. Individuals can and do have huge effects on society. For example, in the United States, Marva Collins had an amazing impact on children previously described as drop-outs; in politics the name most people consider is Nelson Mandela who transformed South Africa; and in business there's a new wave of leaders such as Tony Hsieh changing the way that business works. I describe it as a 'new wave', but of course there have always been inspirational leaders.

On a typical working day, many of us spend a third of our time at work (Figure 0.3). Of course many people spend significantly more than eight hours a day at work. However long we spend, many people experience pressure to become increasingly effective at work.

FIGURE 0.3   Time spent at work

Perhaps these pressures are imposed on us – for example, to get more done – or sometimes they're self-imposed, perhaps by a personal sense of pride or achievement. You might be working towards a promotion, or there might be other reasons. For most people, when we have a great day at work our positive emotions influence 'other' bits of our life too: perhaps we walk from the office with a smile or a bit more bounce in our step. I've also noticed that these emotions often have a contagious effect on those around us, and this is supported by research (Fowler and Christakis, 2009). So while there is still the rent and bills to pay, the question this book seeks to answer is:

How do I get more great days at work?

Foundations in psychology

The basis of this book is 'scientific'. Its roots are in psychology with a strong element of empirically tested research.

Given my experience of training and coaching others, occasionally I've included examples which may highlight a particular point. However, I want the 'stars' of the book to be the evidence provided by specific pieces of research. Therefore I have included references to more information mainly so that you can see the evidence, and explore topics further. Typically within the main body of the book, I've included the author(s) of key pieces of research so you can find out more if you wish, or just skip over them if they're not of interest to you at this time.

If you do decide you'd like to investigate some of the research further, and if reading and understanding psychological research is new to you, I recommend *How to Think Straight About Psychology* (Stanovich, 2010). It's easy to see gaps in single studies but often it's the body of evidence which provides support for theories. It's too easy to dismiss research because the sample of people who have been observed as part of the research do not resemble the people you're typically working with. However, Stanovich addresses all these questions clearly and provides a good foundation on which to start your reading of the more technical research papers – although a number of leading academics have also written popular science books, which I've also referenced.

Psychology

There has been interest in the workings of the mind for millennia, and psychology as a science is a discipline which has been in existence for over 100 years. However, until about 10 years ago the *majority* of the focus of this science had been on reducing the symptoms of mental illness (eg depression, anxiety). Sometimes traditional psychology was described as the journey of taking an individual from –5 to 0 (from ill to OK). This type of psychology is perhaps not something traditionally of interest to a healthy business professional.

Of course there have always been exceptions, like 'sports psychology', and there have always been scientists and researchers interested in how humans flourish, but often these researchers were in disparate disconnected disciplines, such as motivation, healthy ageing, developing resilience or finding the benefits of positive emotions. Disparate, until they started to be grouped in a discipline known as *positive psychology*.

Positive psychology

Positive psychology is the term that's now commonly used for the study of human flourishing, or what takes a person on the theoretical journey from 0 to +5 (from OK to flourishing).

Research now included under the banner of positive psychology includes: research around motivation; what constitutes well-being; and there's some fascinating research around the study of memory and choosing our time perspectives. There's research on different types of goal setting, and studies that demonstrate that solution-focused coaching combined with positive emotions is the most effective type of coaching (Grant, 2006).

Furthermore, recent neuroscience research shows that the brain can and does develop and change, so it's never too late to learn new skills and to have great days at work. If you're even slightly curious about how findings from the science of psychology impact on work, or if you're short of time but have an interest in what the field of positive psychology has for you, then this book will kick-start your learning as it distils some of the key research and applies it to the context of work.

Why positive psychology hasn't had more traction in the business world

Positive psychology has earned the reputation as the study of happiness, and as such has sometimes been a little removed from the serious professional. Although the interventions from positive psychology are well researched, with terminology such as 'counting one's blessings' and keeping a 'gratitude diary', business can be forgiven for thinking that it's 'nice', although a bit 'fluffy' with no place in the business world. My intention in writing this book is to highlight the application of relevant science to business professionals. Having trained and coached others, I personally think there's a huge relevance for business professionals.

For most people, when they think of a great day at work, they recall examples of what they and their teams overcame to achieve significant results. The individual is motivated and engaged. What organization doesn't want a team of motivated professionals? Gallup research has demonstrated that motivated employees have a direct impact on the business's bottom line. This could sound like manipulation until one remembers the negative impact of stress.

Having great days at work brings both physical and health benefits to the individual. Being more engaged in work is likely to bring a state of flow and motivation – whilst the flow state can be found in both sporting and leisure activities it's most common in the workplace. Flow is important for our mental well-being (more on this can be found in Chapter 5).

Effective use of time perspectives leads not only to increases in well-being but also in business effectiveness – understanding when to look back and when to look forward sounds too simplistic, but can be at the centre of many a protracted and inefficient meeting.

The research around achievement shows it is an important part of motivation – and as long as individuals are achieving goals which are in line with the priorities of the business then this will lead to business effectiveness.

Two sides of the same coin

I'm not so sure that a clear delineation exists between psychology and positive psychology; in my opinion they are two sides of the same coin. In recent years there has been much focus on the 'positive' of positive psychology, which historically has been an area somewhat neglected by research. However, I wouldn't want to discount the value found in the significant body of 'traditional' psychological research.

I present some of the fascinating research from positive psychology to a broader readership because much of it has been locked away in academia, or has been adopted by a more 'self-help' audience. However, with my corporate training and coaching experience I see a huge value in bringing this material to a professional audience. My background in transactional analysis psychotherapy will provide a strong underpinning.

DEFINITIONS

Psychotherapy: is a general term referring to therapeutic interaction or treatment contracted between a trained professional and a client, patient, family, couple or group.

Psychology: is an academic and applied discipline that involves the scientific study of mental functions and behaviours.

Positive psychology: seeks 'to find and nurture genius and talent', and 'to make normal life more fulfilling', rather than merely treating mental illness.

Source: Wikipedia

It's more than positive thinking

I'm often asked if positive psychology is positive thinking, and my answer is both yes and no.

Why 'no'?

Positive psychology is not just positive thinking. I often fear that thinking positively denies the reality of the situation. At an extreme, I think that *just* thinking positively can be slightly delusional. Taken to extremes, if a person were on the *Titanic* in the aftermath of hitting an iceberg, thinking positively would not change the *situation*. However, hiding in one's cabin expecting the worst is also not likely to give you the motivation to get out and hunt for the life rafts. Ignoring problems – and simple wishful thinking – is not positive psychology.

In my opinion, positive thinking has to be combined with both understanding the reality and implications of the situation and taking action(s).

Why 'yes'?

Positive psychology is about thinking positively. It is about expecting to find a way through a situation and being active in your efforts. In the above example of the *Titanic*, positive thinking is thinking there will be life rafts and searching for them.

Often in any situation there is a range of ways to explain events and the motives of yourself and others. Our patterns of thinking about these events can become automatic or habitual, and we may not even notice patterns in our own thinking. Often it's easier to notice other people's thinking patterns: 'so-and-so is a bit negative, can always find the cloud in every silver lining'. Various pieces of empirical research show that we can start to pay attention to our own thinking patterns and, should we wish to, start to change them.

The way we think, store and remember events affects our experience in the world. Not only can we change our experiences, but we can also change how we remember our experiences – which could be described as positive thinking.

Positive psychology in action

For example, Philip Zimbardo's (Zimbardo and Boyd, 2008) research shows that we each focus on different perspectives of time. Some people focus more on the past, and others on the future, and some people are more focused on the now. Ilona Boniwell and her colleagues (2010) noted that those people who could have a 'balanced time perspective' – that is those who were able to focus on good things about the past, enjoy the present, as well as having goals in the future – were more likely to experience higher levels of well-being. The good news is that there are several things that you can do to improve your ability in any of the time perspectives, eg you can learn to 'savour' a past experience. We will explore how to do this in Chapter 5.

Another example: Laura King and her colleagues (King *et al*, 2000) found that even when individuals had experienced adversity, when they were able to find benefit from the situation by changing how they thought about it their experience of the situation changed. The team researched parents of Down's Syndrome children, and found that those who (ultimately) found benefit in the traumatic event were happier than those who didn't. King used the expression 'the hard road to the good life'. She found that where the parents of Down's Syndrome children told stories that involved elements of struggle and overcoming adversity this led to personal growth. Positive psychology is not just about the focus on the positive but also about building resilience to handle adversity. If benefit finding can be used in these highly personal situations, how can we use it within the business environment?

In *Great Days at Work* I present a framework to provide you with a context for describing the 'things you can do' which will contribute to you having more great days at work. These 'things you can do' have often been scientifically researched and are described as 'interventions'. *Great Days at Work* provides a framework for you to get the most out of these interventions.

1
The great days framework

Positive psychology interventions have been scientifically established as effective. Just follow them, and you will experience benefits. The interventions are very simple; for example, there's a positive psychology intervention called 'three good things'. Essentially all that's required is for you, prior to going to sleep, to briefly write about three good things that have happened to you during the day. That's it. For many people it sounds too simplistic to be effective, so they don't start it. When I work with clients, I provide a framework so that the interventions make more logical sense, and address some of the nagging questions and doubts that I've found people experience before starting them.

For example, when talking about the 'three good things' intervention, if I start to tell you that it's a way of 'reprogramming' the brain to notice the good events, you might start to be a bit more interested. As I talk about reprogramming you might question whether as adults our brains really can be reprogrammed. Therefore, it is useful for me to describe some of the latest brain and neuroplasticity research, and recent findings about our abilities as adults to learn. You may not be totally enthralled by the idea of your brain being reprogrammed – and that's OK too. If that's the case you'll be pleased to know that this book alone is not enough to do any reprogramming – that requires at least some effort on your part – so feel free to read without commitment to making changes and to cherry-pick the ideas that take your fancy.

There is a breadth of research in positive psychology and many of the topics I will cover, which lead to great days at work, are intertwined. Figure 1.1 shows the framework that I've developed from the latest research findings and is based on my experience of training and coaching thousands of people. The structure I've developed is designed to be logical, easy to follow and use.

The great days framework – at a glance

FIGURE 1.1   The great days at work framework

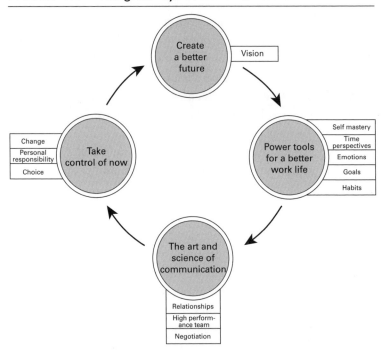

In the remainder of this chapter I provide an overview of the framework, and if you're the type of person that prefers to dip into sections of a book rather than read from cover to cover, my recommendation would be to read the rest of this chapter first to get an understanding of how the sections are related, and then dip in!

Overview

Great Days at Work is arranged in four parts after Chapter 1. The first part (Chapters 2 and 3) encourages you to **take control of now**. It puts you in the driving rather than the passenger seat on the bus of life.

Once you're in the driving seat, it's useful to know where you're heading, so the second part (Chapter 4) works to create your vision, so that you can **create a better future**.

The third part (Chapters 5 to 9) gives you some **power tools for a better work life**. These tools will enable you to make changes, from tweaks and minor modifications to larger changes, all of which will give you more great days at work.

The fourth and final part (Chapters 10 to 12) recognizes that when you're at work there are other people. These others can either be the grit and niggle in your work day or can enhance the experience. This section, **the art and science of communications**, gives you approaches to enhance the experience of working with others.

Take control of now

This part really is about putting you in the driving seat, giving you the reins and showing you it's never too late to have great days at work.

Change

In order to have great days at work, you'll need to take control. It may require you to do some things differently, necessitating some form of change. In this initial part I set the scene for change. There used to be a belief that after we reach the age of about 18 our brains stop developing. However, research shows that our brains continue to develop – albeit at a slower pace than children's. If brains have the capacity to grow, the things that then hold people back from learning are either their thoughts (sometimes described as self-limiting beliefs) or their approach to learning. Chapter 2 explores the three elements of change: brains, thoughts or mindset and the process of change.

Brains: First I'll simply and briefly highlight some recent studies on neuroscience and brain plasticity. This might sound a bit heavy, but it clearly demonstrates that contrary to what was popular belief, the brain continues to grow and develop, creating new pathways. This is important because it does mean you can learn new skills, habits and attitudes.

Thoughts: What can halt development are people's 'background thoughts'. The way we think is like a computer operating system – most of the time we don't notice it's there. Our background thoughts might be experienced as internal voices (self-talk) that are familiar to us, perhaps they tell us to 'go for it!', or 'don't be so ridiculous!' Sometimes our thinking patterns form well-worn pathways; they are rutted. When someone's thoughts become entrenched they don't give themselves the opportunity to learn new things.

If you hear yourself use words like 'never' or 'always', for example 'I'll never learn that' or 'I always make mistakes with this', this type of phrase gives you clues that your thoughts have become rutted, and it's time for an upgrade to the operating system of your thoughts. Carole Dweck's research on mindset shows that people can change, and that they can learn new skills (Dweck, 2006). There are practical activities on how you can develop a growth mindset, and these are discussed further in Chapter 2.

The process of change: Generally change isn't binary, it's an iterative process which can be unfamiliar to many people. In the same way that we might wish for teleportation to get us from A to B the journey of change isn't instant, from unskilled to skilled. Therefore it is useful to have a map before heading on the journey. An expectation of the bumps in the path could lead to hyper-vigilance and a self-fulfilling prophecy. However, as you'll discover in Chapter 2, most people experience some form of dip in motivation over time on the change journey. With this foresight you have the opportunity to be prepared. With this knowledge, your job is, if possible, to minimize both the depth of the dip and the duration of it. Often knowing about typical challenges in advance means that a different route can be taken, or at least the appropriate tools and support can accompany the traveller on the route!

Personal responsibility

It's too easy to look for reasons why something can't be done, for example, the processes, the systems, the manager or simply lack of time. However, there is real power in the words 'I can ...'. Even with such powerful words there might be limits to the progress that can be made, although generally there is at least *something* that can be done. The skill is to find 'that something' that you're willing to do, and to take action.

In Chapter 3 on personal responsibility I'll take a look at how you can take appropriate personal responsibility in order to make progress. Whilst the specific focus is on having great days at work, this tool can be used in all aspects of your life.

The tool is Covey's (1989) circle of control.[1] It is an effective way of distinguishing what you can and can't control in life. Its power as a decision-making tool is that it enables you to focus on what you can control, and begin to let go of what you can't. In Chapter 3 we will take an in-depth look at this tool and how you can use it. The tool gives a fresh perspective on how you choose to spend your valuable resources of both energy and time.

Choice

Throughout the course of this book I will debunk several popular assumptions that the research doesn't support which will allow you to make better decisions. The first of these popular myths that I'll tackle is around choice.

Many of us like to think that we have choice and autonomy both in work and in life, and that choice is a good thing – but actually options can be detrimental to our enjoyment of work and life.

One thing that can stop us making clear choices is wanting to keep our options open – it seems that this is a very natural instinct, but apparently not that useful. Without making clear and active choices there is no going forward. We become more like a rudderless ship blown by the winds of fate and carried by the tides of destiny.

Having begun to explore why and how it's useful to narrow your options, I'll then invite you to put pen to paper to explore and define your own vision.

Create a better future

> *The best way to predict the future is to create it.*
>
> Abraham Lincoln

Vision

Vision is essentially long-range goal setting. Organizations can have a vision. However, the focus of this book is creating your personal vision. For some people the process of setting and having a vision can start to define some fundamental questions around what's important to them.

Knowing what's personally important begins to tap into what's described as 'intrinsic motivation'. Intrinsic motivation refers to motivation that comes from inside an individual rather than from any external or outside rewards, such as money or grades. If you've ever had the experience of being intrinsically motivated you will know what a powerhouse of energy it is (Ryan and Deci, 2000). For many, creating a vision is not an overnight process. There can be a number of inputs and Chapter 4 will give you practical activities in order to begin the process of creating your vision. One important aspect is knowing your values.

Chapter 4 on vision will explore the importance of knowing your values. Whereas your vision is in the future, your values are what are important to you right now. The process of becoming increasingly aware of your values can also influence your vision: as you expand your awareness of what's important to you then you may want to enhance your vision to get more of 'it' in your life.

Your values guide your decision making in 'the now'. Values can be useful in decision making or in situations of internal conflict. You could view your values as providing your compass for navigating through life.

Knowing where you're going and what's important to you are both important aspects of personal effectiveness. They enable achievement and mastery of your work which provides a sense of accomplishment. Knowing the dual aspects of where you are going and what's important to you are the foundations for time management, because it's easier to say 'no' to distractions when you have a clear direction.

Power tools for a better work life

You have a number of power tools available to you to change your experience of work. Unlike regular power tools, these power tools are free and aren't kept in the shed at the bottom of the garden or at the back of the overfilled cupboard under the stairs – both are awkward to get at, and too much bother most of the time. The power tools that I will introduce you to are yours, and they're available for you whenever you need them.

A different analogy is that of the humble office chair. Typically office chairs have levers to adjust the height and back support. I've noticed that some people don't know that the levers are there, so sit awkwardly. Some know the levers are there and don't bother to use them to increase their comfort. Others actively adjust their chair to make it comfortable. I'd like to compel you to use the last option. Actively use power tools for your benefit.

These power tools have great, easy-to-use functionality which many people either aren't aware of or overlook. There are two tools, each with different settings. The first is time travel, or the ability to change your time perspective. It's as easy as switching from thinking about what you had for breakfast yesterday, to contemplating what you'll be doing later. The second tool is emotions – again the switch is easy.

Time travel

I've seen much time wasted in business by focusing on the past (what happened) when it would be more productive to spend time focused on the future: what are the options we could take, or what's the solution? Whilst the skill of time travel in business is key to increased productivity, it really comes into its own when developing great days.

Essentially the skill of 'time travel' is being able to observe and switch your perspective or orientation regarding time. The concept of time travel is adapted from Zimbardo and Boyd's (2008) work on time perspectives, and the importance of having a balanced time perspective (Boniwell *et al*, 2010). Research has shown that we can make changes in those areas which contribute to well-being, and our ability to have great days at work. At the most simple are the time perspectives of past, present and future. However, there are nuances and some specifics around how you can begin to bend time:

- **Present:** when you seek to be totally present and 'in the moment', most of us will notice that thoughts are 'contaminated' by either thoughts from the past or from the future. You can develop your awareness of the present with *mindfulness* (mindfulness meditation).

- **Past:** the goal is to reduce the time and energy you spend having negative thoughts about the past, and for most of us it's to increase the amount of time we spend having positive thoughts about the past.

- **Future:** the future time perspective is about having goals and planning. Often our job has targets to achieve which keeps us future focused, but in our personal life our planning can be far less structured. It is said that a large number of people spend more time planning their summer holiday than they do planning their life, and the goals that will take them in that direction.

Chapter 5 explores how you can time travel to enhance your experience at work and gain perspective on life. Unlike the time travel undertaken by Dr Who, no Tardis is provided.

Use positive emotions to supercharge your life

For many years the overwhelming opinion was that being successful *led* to happiness. It's logical to think that it's easier for someone to be happy *after* they've got the job of their dreams or made their fortune. However, rather counter intuitively, research from the field of positive psychology has shown that positive emotions *lead to* success. Yes, I'll say this again, the *shocking secret* about success and happiness is that success doesn't lead to happiness, happiness leads to success.

So, what's the logic? Happier people naturally attract more opportunities and are in a better frame of mind to make more of these opportunities. Therefore happiness *leads to* success. To prove the point, there's a scientifically proven ratio for the proportion of positive emotions to negative emotions which once reached shows a positive impact on health, well-being and success. Positive emotions range in energy from high energy (eg jumping for joy) to lower energy feelings of contentment, and the good news is that they all count as positive emotions.

Often people feel that they are victims of their emotions, that emotions happen to them and that they lack control. Others have tight and rigid control over their emotions, and think that all that's required in the workplace is a stiff upper lip. Indeed, for most people emotions are generally not considered appropriate in a business environment. This is an important myth that we will debunk!

Chapter 6 will explore some of the research on positive emotions, and specifically what you can do to get more positive emotions in your work–life balance. Chapter 7 looks at goals, the important 'how to's' in terms of achieving your vision.

Smarter decision making

In the chapter on working habits (Chapter 8), I describe how you can continue to embed changes so that they become new habits. Two almost contradictory aspects are explored. Firstly there are small daily decisions that you can automate, which has a two-fold benefit – it becomes easier to do something than not – thus creating a habit. Removing decision making from routine decisions gives you more energy.

Much has been written about the habits of Barack Obama, Steve Jobs and Mark Zuckerberg, and how these successful people limit their choices around non-important aspects of their life. For example, it's reported that Obama has the same breakfast every day. Jobs had a number of identical outfits, as does Zuckerberg. All these things reduce the number of decisions they have to make. We will explore why this might be important later, along with the supporting research evidence.

Secondly, the almost contradictory aspect is of paying attention to your 'background thoughts'. Most of us have thoughts that pop into our minds automatically, often out of our awareness. Changing some of your thinking can change your experience of work. I'll describe some of the research which begins to show the ways in which this automatic thinking can hold you back – and how you can apply this so that it doesn't.

Therefore, in order to have great days at work, I suggest you deliberately pay attention to your background thoughts and see which ones need a 'spring clean'. Think of it like an upgrade of a computer's operating system to a more powerful version that supports your growth and development and enables you to have more great days at work.

Self-mastery

For convenience I've divided Chapter 9 on self-mastery into two sections. Firstly I touch on some physiological aspects of our wellbeing, around sleep, nutrition and exercise. The second aspect is developing insight and self-awareness and an ability to have a range of tools to deal with obstacles.

Many people get benefit by starting with some of the approaches in the self-mastery chapter (Chapter 9), which is the reason why Figure 1.1 is shown with the 'self' column touching the base.

For example, for some people, gaining an understanding of their strengths early may give them more curiosity to have an open mindset. For others, building self-esteem is an important place to start, and it can be done through physical exercise or increased self-awareness. For others, tools to build resilience or to handle difficult situations will come first.

The art and science of communications

Working with others can be either a miserable or joyful experience. I provide some tools to maximize the likelihood that you will experience great days at work, with positive working relationships.

Working with others

The importance of social networks has been cited as an important factor in well-being. In a work environment we don't often get to choose our colleagues so Chapter 10 looks at some of the tools to develop more effective relationships. Then we look at how these skills are applied both to creating high-performing teams (Chapter 11) and in negotiations (Chapter 12).

Let's get started

You may wonder if it's possible to learn new ways of relating to other people. The next chapter (Chapter 2) begins by exploring whether we can as adults change and learn new ways of being, and ultimately new ways of communicating with others.

Note

1   There are a number of scientific terms related to the concept of circle of control. In some respects this is linked to the positive psychology term 'hope' – of having *agency* and *pathways* to solve a problem. The scientific research is around *locus of control*.

Part One
TAKE CONTROL
OF NOW

2
Change – adapt to thrive

He who rejects change is the architect of decay.
The only human institution which rejects progress is
the cemetery.

Harold Wilson

Although the box below contains a joke, I hope it demonstrates how quickly new information can change a person's understanding, and therefore change their course (of action).

US ship: Please divert your course 0.5 degrees to the south to avoid a collision.

Canadian reply: Recommend you divert your course 15 degrees to the south to avoid a collision.

US ship: This is the Captain of a US Navy ship. I say again, divert your course.

Canadian reply: No. I say again, you divert YOUR course!

US ship: THIS IS THE AIRCRAFT CARRIER USS CORAL SEA. WE ARE A LARGE WARSHIP OF THE US NAVY. DIVERT YOUR COURSE NOW!!

Canadian reply: This is a lighthouse. Your call.

Brains change

'Brain science' has shown that brains can continue to develop and make new neural networks. Neuroplasticity is the term used to describe changes in the brain that occur in response to experience. There are different ways that the brain can change, from growing new connections to the creation of new neurons. One of the ways in which changes in brain function patterns are assessed is with functional magnetic resonance imaging (fMRI), commonly known as an MRI scan. The colourful pictures that are produced as a result of an MRI scan show the different areas of brain activity.

Often MRI scans are used within the medical profession to detect problems with the brain, but MRI scans have also been used to investigate specific changes and activities that occur when learning new skills, and have shown that changes do take place. Scientists at the Waisman Laboratory for Brain Imaging and Behavior investigated meditating. They show that 'the mental training of meditation is fundamentally no different from any other form of skill acquisition that can induce plastic changes in the brain' (Davidson and Lutz, 2008).

So whilst there was once a belief that as adults our brains were 'fully developed', more recent research suggests that brains physically continue to make new connections through adulthood, ie brains are dynamic and not static.

Is your brain wired for growth?

There's an oft-used statement of Henry Ford's: 'Whether you think you can or whether you think you can't you're right.' There is much truth in the statement, and it does seem that even though our brains are capable of growth, our thoughts can become self-fulfilling prophecies and so either promote or stifle growth. Whatever you choose to believe, choose carefully.

For example, suppose a person thinks they're 'no good at presentations'. Not surprisingly they don't volunteer for presentations, indeed they may actively avoid presenting. All the time they're not practising they're not getting any better or any less fearful at presenting ... so it's no wonder giving 'poor presentations' becomes self-fulfilling.

Research has found that one of the primary things that can hold back learning and developing new connections in the brain is having a 'fixed mindset'.

Mindset overview

Carole Dweck, researcher and author of *Mindset* (2006), found that our attitude can be fundamental to our success. I think that the really brilliant and inspiring piece from Dweck's research is the finding that whatever your current mindset, changes to attitudes *are* possible! Dweck initially found that there were different interpretations of the word 'ability', which led to a person's energy being targeted in different directions.

Take a moment, think of a work situation and consider which of the following two statements you believe is truer for you:

- I have some great abilities which I constantly prove both to myself and others.
- I'm constantly learning, and increasing my ability.

If you're not sure which applies to you, reflect on your thoughts around mistakes and failures. Where do you spend your effort? Do you spend your time 'proving' your excellent skills and abilities to others, or do you find opportunities to make mistakes, an inevitable part of learning new skills and growing?

The former statement is more strongly linked to having a *fixed* mindset. The latter statement is more linked to a *growth* mindset. You might wonder why this matters. It's because with a fixed mindset we want to maintain the status quo. Dweck describes how when we adopt a fixed mindset we become non-learners, whereas with a growth mindset, we seek new opportunities and learn and grow from them. The growth mindset is the attitude of people who learn from their mistakes and remain open to new information and are curious.

By considering the following questions, you will probably reach a similar conclusion; in order to remain successful over time you will need to seek a growth mindset:

- How much new information do you think a person can assimilate when they're specifically looking for evidence to support their views?
- What do you think the risk is for a person who's not open to new information?
- How consistently will a person have great days if they're constantly looking at reinforcing their ego?

The limitations of a fixed mindset

It's not that a fixed mindset is 'bad' and a growth mindset is 'good' – there are different implications to adopting each mindset. It's useful to remember that it's not the person that's fixed but an attitude, and this attitude is context dependent. Dweck's research found that whilst people with a fixed mindset can succeed, it's typically those with a growth mindset that remain successful over time.

When a person has a fixed mindset they are constantly looking to reinforce their views of the world. They look to be 'right', which might prevent them from collaborating or learning something new, or even resisting inevitable change. In the same way that King Canute couldn't hold back the tide, change is inevitable and will happen with or without you.

At an extreme the behaviour that comes with a fixed mindset can lead to isolation from colleagues. There is something to be said for being an expert, but who wants to continually work with a 'know-it-all' who never takes others' ideas on board?

The implications of having a fixed mindset are that you don't have to take in new information, and you avoid new challenges, almost as if you want to stop time. A fixed mindset can exacerbate underlying fears, such as fear of failure, a fear of not being 'successful', or a fear of losing the success you've already achieved.

Essentially what I'm suggesting is that it's *no fun* having a fixed mindset. Underlying the fixed mindset are fears: these may not be fully articulated but they underpin the fixed mindset. For example, working with others can be perceived as a threat (if others might have more knowledge than me and might dismiss my ideas, I have to be 'on guard' and defensive at all times).

Finally, another 'price' of having a fixed mindset is that while you are constantly seeking to reinforce your ego, views and opinions, you are making it more difficult, if not impossible, to see new opportunities.

The growth mindset

Contrast the limitations of the fixed mindset with a growth mindset. With the growth mindset, new opportunities will be viewed positively as a way to stretch and develop your skills. Adopting a growth mindset will contribute to you having great days at work.

Constant stretching of one's skills might sound like continuous hard work, but in his seminal work on 'flow' Csikszentmihalyi (2002) found that the state of flow, a sense of timeless absorption in a task, is achieved by increasing the level of skills alongside the level of challenge. Whilst it may not be surprising to know that the state of flow happens in many contexts from engaging in sports to music, it probably is surprising that his research found that the most flow occurs at work. I'll describe more about the concept of flow and how to achieve increased levels of flow in more detail in Chapter 5.

A growth mindset and will enable you to be more willing to try new things and learn from the experience, which is more likely to build on your existing skills so that you develop mastery. The concept of mastery is another important building block of intrinsic motivation. Ultimately you will be more satisfied and grow as a person and typically will be more successful ... a rather nice side-effect.

I studied manufacturing processes over 20 years ago at university, and I remember the encouragement to keep an open mind. This was supported with a cautionary tale about the humble milk bottle.

There was a time in the UK when the majority of people had their milk delivered by someone driving an electric milk float. Milk was delivered in glass bottles, empties were returned and recycled.

There was an ongoing manufacturing quest to find a lighter yet more durable glass bottle. The focus was on changing the shape of the bottle and adjusting the density of the glass. In the meantime, the milk packaging market had moved on to Tetra Paks and plastic bottles, and the glass milk bottle all but disappeared.

The lesson I took from this was to keep scanning the broader environment so as not to miss out on new information or new technologies which change the face of the industry.

Being open to change stood me in good stead. I trained to work in the manufacturing industry, but following the economic decline in manufacturing, the fact that I was open to new opportunities led me first to Information Technology, before finding and pursuing my passion for developing others and seeing them thrive.

You have both fixed and growth mindsets

The same person can have both a fixed and a growth mindset: it just depends on the context or situation. This is good news because even if you notice that in many situations you predominantly use a fixed mindset, it's highly likely that in some areas of your life you'll have a growth mindset. Therefore you already know what it's like to have a growth mindset in different situations. The first step is to be clear about what it's like, and then you can switch into 'doing' growth mindset behaviours, even if at the beginning it's not natural.

Do you have to switch into the growth mindset?

You may have heard of Viktor Frankl, a holocaust survivor. In his book *Man's Search for Meaning* he wrote: 'The one thing you can't take away from me is the way I choose to respond to what you do to me. The last of one's freedoms is to choose one's attitude in any given circumstance.' So, changing how you think is up to you. *You* are in control of that. Therefore the answer to the question 'Must I change my mindset?' is an emphatic no! However, you do have the power of choice of whether to, and how to, react in any given situation.

My intention in putting mindsets early on in the book is so that you can take heart if you find your thinking is 'stuck', and find yourself saying 'I can't change' or 'I'm not the type of person who ...'. Then you can remember that *the first thing you can change is your mindset*. In fact as a foundation piece if you only take one thing, that's it – you can change your mindset.

Perhaps there are times when there's significant growth in several areas of life, then we might *choose* not to grow in some other areas. However, I would encourage you to review the decision perhaps every couple of months, to check that your mindset is still serving you. You don't have to become a slave to your past decisions, just as you don't have to let your current mindset define you.

For many years I've had a fixed mindset about cooking ('I can't'). However, I recently updated my mindset, and started to try out a new set of recipes. I found it time consuming, so I took an active decision that given my 'growth mindset' in other areas of my life (like becoming an author), I thought I'd leave the culinary experimentation for now! So even though I choose not to practise at the moment, I know I can. I've thus changed my mindset and am more open to learning how to cook.

Which mindset are you using?

How can you spot your growth mindset? Take a look at different aspects of your life. Perhaps at work you like to get things 'right' (an indicator of a fixed mindset), but on the golf course you're more likely to recognize that you can constantly improve, aiming to lower your handicap. Perhaps in the golfing environment you occasionally take some lessons or get coaching from someone who makes suggestions on how to improve your swing. Perhaps some of your learning comes from books on or around the golfing topic, whether it's *The Inner Game of Golf* (Gallwey, 1996) or a practical *Your Perfect Swing* (Suttie, 2006). Alternatively perhaps you have a mentor or friend who can give you top tips (which you go on to test for yourself). All of these are sure signs of a growth mindset. In this environment you recognize that sometimes when you make an adjustment there's an element of going backwards before making a leap in improvement.

How to change your mindset

FIGURE 2.1   Changing your mindset

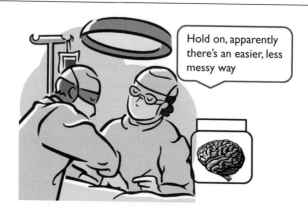

If you want to change your mindset, then follow these proven steps.

ACTIVITY   Changing your mindset

- First take a moment to remind yourself of a situation where you already have a *growth mindset*. If at first a situation doesn't readily come to mind think about different aspects of your life.
- What's the situation? Picture yourself in the situation.
- When you're making mistakes while learning, what do you say to yourself? How do you feel? What are your thoughts?
- How do you encourage yourself?
- How do you feel when you succeed? What are your thoughts? What do you say to yourself?
- What do you say to yourself when contemplating the next challenge? What thoughts/feelings propel you forward?
- Take a moment as you finish that activity to jot down a few notes: what are your empowering thoughts? What do you say to yourself to encourage and motivate yourself?

You now have a snapshot of how you learn when you have a growth mindset. You can deliberately use it if you notice your mindset is closing. Force yourself to do what you do when you're in a growth mindset. But even with your own recipe, applying it to a new situation can be a challenge for some people. I've noticed that having a recipe or template is the second stage, and there's typically a first stage of clearing out unhelpful beliefs that haven't been updated.

Underlying beliefs

The fixed mindset is a symptom of underlying beliefs in a particular area. When a person has a fixed mindset typically their internal dialogue (the little voices in their head) can be inaccurate. For example their thoughts may be: self-attack, 'I am so stupid ... why did I say that in front of the boss?'; catastrophization, 'Oh ... I will never get promoted and will end up in some dead end job, and ... etc'; or generalization, 'They always say that'.

For someone with a fixed mindset playing golf, a poor swing might elicit an internal dialogue: 'I'll never be any good' or 'Duh, how stupid'. Of course this is just an example – everyone's internal dialogue is different.

Whenever you find your internal dialogue is not supportive, take notice and start to think about the effects, both positive and negative, that such dialogue has on you. List both the costs and benefits.

For example, the costs may be that you don't grow and learn new skills. Internal dialogue that's not supportive will often 'cost' you. Who wants their internal voices to tell them that they're a loser, or that they'll never be any good? Perhaps a fear of looking 'stupid' might mean that you do not even consider, let alone seize, opportunities that you perceive might put at risk your 'status as expert'. You may not be fully tuned into your internal dialogue, so you may want to consider whether an outsider would see you 'playing it safe' by continuing to be the expert ... or would they see you learning new things, and making mistakes in the process? Both are ok.

There could be some benefits of holding inaccurate beliefs. As the expert, you don't ever feel foolish by not knowing. You may enjoy people coming to you to ask your advice. You may not take risks and therefore stay in your comfort zone, you stay expert in your field and only receive positive recognition. However, this rarely lasts for long: the world passes you by as technology and the situation change and you are no longer the guru.

Take five minutes to really think through all the costs and benefits. At the end you can make a decision to change the underlying belief, and to have a growth mindset.

In Chapter 8 we look at the work of Dr Aaron Beck and explore further how you can update unhelpful beliefs, and turn them into things that work *for* you and not against you and your health. But for now you may simply want to weigh up the costs and benefits and contemplate the advantages of changing to a growth mindset.

Growth mindsets can lead to personal growth

Heartening news is that often the attributes associated with the fixed mindset are a stage that people *go through* as part of their natural development. This can be seen more clearly in relation to how people receive feedback.

Receiving feedback

Leadership is typically associated with a formal role; however, there are also informal leaders. Often there is much investment in developing leaders, not least of all because leaders are invested to develop their teams. However, not all leaders are the same. A number of approaches show there are distinct developmental stages associated with leadership development (Rooke and Torbert, 2005; Beck and Cowan, 2006).

Although there are a range of differences in how a leader behaves at each of the stages, one of the relevant differentiators in the context of mindset is a person's openness to feedback (Cook-Greuter, 2004). In the box on page 35 you can see that the less-developed leaders 'reject feedback, externalise blame and retaliate harshly'. Whereas, *typically* the more 'developed' leaders (which may or may not equate to seniority) are encouraging and welcoming of feedback as they see the comments as an opportunity to grow.

How understanding and response to feedback change with increasing development

Magician: Views feedback (loops) as a natural part of living systems, essential for learning and change, but takes them with a grain of salt

Strategist: Invites feedback for self-actualization, conflict is seen as an inevitable aspect of viable and multiple relationships

Individualist: Welcomes feedback as necessary for self-knowledge and to uncover hidden aspects of their own behaviour

Achiever: Accepts feedback, especially if it helps them to achieve their goals and to improve

Expert: Takes feedback personally, defends own position, dismisses feedback from those who are not seen as experts in the same field (general manager)

Diplomat: Receives feedback as disapproval, or as a reminder of norms

Opportunist: Reacts to feedback as an attack or threat

Source: Cook-Greuter (2004)

You might be part of an organization that has formal systems in place for gathering feedback, not just from supervisors, but often from peers and subordinates too. Often these systems are linked to recognition and reward systems – ie whether or not you'll get a salary increase – and this can lead 'feedback' to be a very emotive topic. For many people the connection between feedback and salary makes it harder to be objective about the feedback and think longer term about possible changes as a result, knowing the direct and imminent impact it will have on salary.

Therefore, put the formal appraisal systems to one side for a moment and consider how you respond to feedback in more informal settings. Of course not all feedback requires any or immediate change as a result. There is an expression that all feedback contains a grain of truth, however badly delivered. Consider feedback you've received in the past: how willing have you been to take on board the information, recognize you have a choice as to what to do next and, if relevant, make changes to your behaviour?

Realizing that you *can* adopt a growth mindset means that from now on you can choose which mindset to put on in any given situation.

It may take some practice – it can feel awkward – just like the person making alterations to their golf swing, but you will be rewarded: dedication to practice will give you more great days at work.

When practising anything new it can be useful to *recognize* and *praise* your own *efforts*, and *celebrate* your own *successes* along the way, which can help in establishing the new habits you're developing. It's likely that there are three pieces of controversy in that statement: acknowledging efforts (rather than results), praising yourself, and in the UK it's slightly counter cultural to celebrate one's own success. These are discussed in turn below.

Recognizing 'efforts'

In a results-orientated environment 'recognizing efforts' is not the norm – and certainly 'praising efforts' is not the British thing to do!

I've spent 15 years working in a multinational IT organization where *results matter*. In fact effort that is not clearly linked to results or somebody's 'scorecard' is often discounted by organizations. Consequently the company's performance measurement system is results orientated. As a manager I've been guilty of focusing on, and measuring, results. These results-orientated workplaces unwittingly encourage a 'fixed' mindset. They don't typically encourage people to learn new skills (in case the results drop), they don't encourage people to do things differently (in case there's a dip in results), they encourage people to repeat the same tasks rather than developing new skills or making innovations.

If you're in a results-orientated work environment, a focus on a growth mindset can sometimes feel like you're swimming against the tide of culture. Other people may not recognize or appreciate the switch in mindset you're making and it's likely that most people won't make a seamless and instantaneous switch from fixed to growth mindset, so here are some suggestions.

You have to notice the micro-changes that you make, and the effort which goes into your own increased awareness: this is a journey. Therefore, in order to support your change to a growth mindset, praise your efforts – recognize you are putting in effort. Results may not be visible – at least initially – but you have to maintain the momentum through the sticky bits in the middle.

The phrase to remember is 'all change in the middle looks like failure' (it's attributed to Professor Kanter of the Harvard Business School and I've occasionally seen this described as Kanter's law). Indeed, Seth Godin wrote a book, *The Dip* (2007), focusing on the middle. It's a quick read with some good strategies; well worth reading.

Learning is not binary

Sometimes we forget that learning is a process not a switch. As a trainer for many years I've noticed that people often expect to learn a new skill instantly. Learning's typically not like that. An oft-used tool in training which demonstrates the movement from 'unconscious incompetence' through to 'unconscious competence' is the four stages of learning, shown in Figure 2.2. It can be useful when learning anything new to remember that 'mastery' of a new skill does not immediately follow learning a new skill. Therefore go kindly on yourself when expectations of mastery do not quite meet your current performance levels.

FIGURE 2.2   The four stages of learning

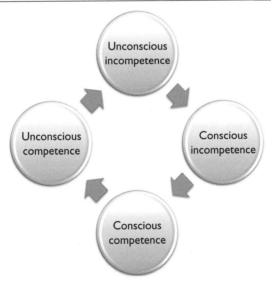

Adapted from Gordon Training International: Learning a new skill is easier said than done

Given that this is such a useful model, let's take a deeper look.

Typically the model starts with *unconscious incompetence*. Take the example of 'giving a presentation'. The first time ever a person presents, it's possible that they might be 'gung-ho' about their expectation. They deliver the presentation with no awareness of the impact it has on their audience. Assuming the person is 'normal' it's likely that there is room for improvement of which they are probably initially unaware.

However, when they have the experience of giving the presentation – perhaps it seemed harder than they'd imagined, maybe they hadn't accounted for nerves, or some of the questions they were asked or the use of the technology. Or perhaps they became aware of some of the complexities of keeping an audience engaged. From this experience the person could become aware that presenting is harder than it seems. As their awareness increases they are aware that they don't know everything, and still have more to learn. They become *consciously incompetent*.

Over time a person can learn to present with planning, focused concentration and deliberation (*consciously competent*). As skills and confidence increase the presenter can more easily present on their topic without thinking. The skill becomes automatic, they become *unconsciously competent* in the skill.

However, the presenter may want to take their skills to the 'next level' and may take further training or coaching, which will involve them doing some aspects of the presentation differently, thus starting the learning cycle again. For example, perhaps they want to use their entire being to tell the story and not have a reliance on slides. In these specific new skills, this may take them from unconscious incompetence – from it being out of awareness that a presentation is more than slides – through to conscious incompetence, 'I didn't know that could be done! How do I do it?'

Being aware of the way in which we learn can help to normalize the experience of learning, and therefore make it less stressful.

When we're unconsciously incompetent at a skill, often failure is outside our awareness. With heightened awareness the individual is more attuned to their 'failures'. The good news is that this knowledge allows them the chance to do something differently, to praise their efforts and awareness and ultimately to improve. Awareness of their failure is not 'bad'. 'Failure' has an important role in the learning process and self-development. Without the awareness that something is failing, a person may not do anything differently to grow or improve the situation.

Praising yourself

You might wish that your team leader, manager or co-workers both notice, and praise any changes that you make to your mindset. However, I have to be honest with you, it is unlikely to happen – at least in the early stages. They may not notice any positive changes in the early stages (see Kanter's law, p 37), as much of the change is going on in your head and attitude, and there's not much to see externally. Furthermore, we become accustomed to other people's ways of behaving. If other people have expectations or assumptions about the way you behave, these assumptions can sometimes override reality. If they do notice something, it's too easy to assume it's a 'quirk' and 'situation normal' will return 'tomorrow'.

However, don't let others' lack of noticing or praising put you off! Eventually there will be external changes to notice and recognition may follow, and if it doesn't you will have grown and have more success – which will feed your intrinsic motivation (discussed later). I recommend that *you* notice *and* positively reinforce both your *efforts* to change *as well as* your achievements, however small, through 'self-praise'. While you can switch your mindset in an instant, maintaining it may take a little more effort. To support this, in Chapter 8 I'll cover how to make more permanent changes to your habits.

How to praise yourself

Whilst it initially might feel unnatural, praising yourself is really very simple to do. As you take action, be supportive in what you tell yourself, in the same way as you would be supportive of a good friend learning something new. Just remember, self-talk is not a replacement to taking action.

So why is positive self-talk important? There is a scientific basis for this self-talk. In the 1970s a psychologist, Meichenbaum (2009), pioneered self-instructional, or encouraging, 'self-talk'. This approach focuses on changing what people say to themselves, both internally and out loud. It is based on the belief that an individual's actions follow directly from this self-talk. Andy Murray attributes positive self-talk to his first grand slam win at the US open (*The Times Magazine*, 30/3/13).

Celebrate success

You put in effort and begin to learn new skills, and you begin to praise yourself for both the effort and the small changes that perhaps only you have noticed. And then you have a larger success. You've experienced the effort it takes to get you there, and therefore it sometimes doesn't feel like it warrants celebrating. It does. As human beings we like pleasure. It's been found that given a choice, animals have been found to prioritize pleasure over food (Olds and Milner, 1954). By not celebrating, we're denying ourselves positive emotions which are good for us (more on this in Chapter 6). Sometimes we're too focused on the next, larger success – but by taking a moment to celebrate, the positive emotions build our resilience, which can keep us fuelled for the next journey of effort.

Typical stages of change

There's no such thing as bad weather in Scotland, only inappropriate clothing.

Billy Connolly

Events happen, and it's how we deal with them that makes a difference. In this section I will describe some of the typical emotions that people go through on change journeys. There is a supporting section in Chapter 9 which explores how you can cope better with a broad range of negative life events. I think this could be useful for you to anticipate likely responses to change. Some of the training work I've done with an organization's leadership undergoing significant change (acquisition) has demonstrated to me the value in

FIGURE 2.3   Four responses to change

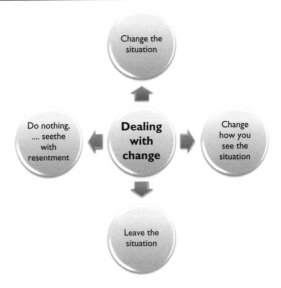

being explicit with this information. Even when the change is positive, individuals can still go through a whole gamut of emotional responses. So knowing that, and being able to take mitigating steps, can help you on your journey.

Alternative responses to change

First of all it's useful to remember that some change is not mandatory. Let's start by acknowledging that in any situation there are different aspects you can change and there are alternative responses other than changing your mind.

Often it doesn't feel as if there are choices in a situation, but generally you're not held hostage to the circumstances and there is a range of ways for you to respond (see Figure 2.3).

1. Change the situation

Frequently there are actions you *can* take to change a situation, and the first step is to think, 'What is the one small thing I can do that will make a positive difference in this situation?' I recognize it's not a phrase that trips off the tongue easily, but it keeps the brain focused on finding solutions.

Many years ago I worked on a large IT project which had a poor reputation based on 'historic' activities. I took up a 'one-woman' campaign to ensure that pretty much everyone I spoke to outside of the project (and who were therefore unaware of the positive changes that were happening) was given the updated positive perspective.

2. Change how you see the situation

In change situations many people automatically fear the worst. Often this fear isn't conscious, more often it's below the surface just 'gnawing away'.

Unfortunately only focusing on the problems will have an effect – and not a positive one. In my work as a coach I've seen people paralysed by the 'fear' of changing, seeing the 'worst' in the potential new situation, without realizing the negative effect of maintaining the status quo.

Perhaps you know someone for whom a small mistake can lead to thinking that snowballs out of control. Although it's rarely said out loud it goes something like: 'The presentation was so bad, my boss will find out, I'll be fired and lose my job. I'll never work again, I won't be able to afford to pay the bills, I'll lose my house, be homeless and my family will desert me.'

The good news is that thinking patterns can be changed. More information on some of the tools to overcome catastrophization can be found in Chapter 5. One of the best ways to approach change is to expect the best outcome in any situation, but also have the tools to effectively deal with any situation, good or bad. However, we should not delude ourselves by setting an unrealistic positive outcome, which can lead to taking unnecessary risks.

I remember some advice given to me by a driving instructor when preparing for my Institute of Advanced Motoring driving assessment. On approaching a roundabout I was advised: 'Prepare to stop, plan to go', which seems good advice for approaching life events.

In Chapter 3 we will explore your focus, and whether you're primed to look for the obstacles or the opportunities. It doesn't matter what your focus has been until now, because you can choose how you see and experience the situation, whether with a welcoming embrace, or keeping it at arm's length – 'no change required here'.

3. Leave the situation

Sometimes we think things will be different if we leave the situation but it depends on what's causing the discomfort.

I remember one acquaintance who found a great job after leaving university – but the initial joy quickly diminished as she found 'every single person' in her office was 'horrible and unprofessional'. She took an active decision to leave the company and find an employer with more professional and nicer employees. You've probably guessed that after an initial honeymoon period with her new employer, to her great distress she found all the new people were not worthy of her exacting standards. So she moved employers again. The lesson is that change often doesn't happen by 'walking away'.

In situations that we don't like, sometimes it can be very tempting to 'walk out', be it a meeting or a job. However, I don't know if you've noticed, but often as a result nothing seems to be different (either for the individual or the organization). Below is an example of the change that happened as a result of an individual leaving the situation. It's a similar example to the one above, but it's from the perspective of the organization as a result of a person leaving:

A colleague gives an example from earlier in her career when she had thought she was indispensable. She describes having to take some extended time off work due to illness (leaving the situation). Upon her return she was disappointed to have found that the world (and the organization) had carried on without her. She realized that leaving a large organization can be like taking your hand out of a bucket of water and seeing the hole that's been left. Everything carries on.

Please note: I'm not suggesting that you should *never* leave a situation. There are times, for either discomfort or growth, when it is time to move on. What I am suggesting though is that you explore your motives and begin by looking first at your attitude and motivation to ensure that the change brings the desired outcome.

Do nothing ... resentment and other emotions

Sometimes on hearing about a forthcoming change people do nothing which is a typical initial response. 'Doing nothing' can quickly be accompanied by 'feelings'. There is a pattern of emotions that people go through as they experience a change in circumstances.

Analysing the emotions of change

There's a common range of emotional responses a person goes through. This is often described as the change curve (see Figure 2.4).

FIGURE 2.4   The change curve

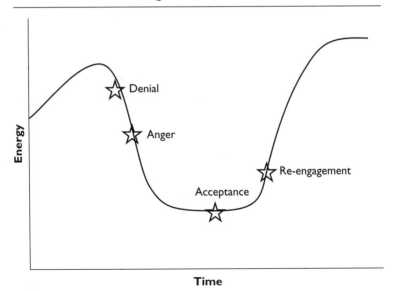

Essentially a typical 'denial' response is ignoring the situation, perhaps hoping or, not believing the change will happen. Anger and resistance are the common next responses – 'How dare they!' By definition, acceptance happens at the low point. Following acceptance is re-engagement and commitment to the change. It's important to note that the sequence of stages can be different for each person, and indeed some people may not experience all of the emotions.

The duration and intensity of the emotion is also likely to be experienced differently depending on the person and the context. As an example of the differences, at one end of the 'anger' spectrum, a person could experience mild feelings of resentment; at the other end someone may experience full blown anger.

In my experience of working with change in organizations, there are several different (although similar) charts showing how a person might typically transition through the stages of change. The role of the professionals involved in leading change is to facilitate how low the dip goes, and to reduce how long it stays low. However, knowing these are natural responses, it's also something you can take responsibility for when managing yourself and your emotions in situations of change. In fact, by being (self-) aware, it will make a change experience less befuddling, even if it doesn't make it any easier.

The good news is that more often than not people grow as a result of the change. Therefore by looking at all change as a growth opportunity, it can make the process more tolerable and increase the likelihood of getting something positive out of it. This is another form of 'growth mindset', which is proactively seeking the positive. This approach is often known as benefit finding, which is covered further in Chapter 5.

Knowing that there is a range of responses which are 'normal' can assist people experiencing change. Resistance is a natural early reaction to change. As you read this book, if you feel resistant to any of the ideas, you might ask yourself whether this in itself is an indication of the early stages of change. This could be great news – resistance is the first step to changing what you do in order to have more great days at work.

Summary

- Your brain continues to develop into adulthood.
- Attitude or mindset can either hold us back or accelerate us going forward.
- There are two different mindsets – fixed and growth.
- You can learn to use and apply a growth mindset in many situations which will enable you to learn, grow and make the most of opportunities.
- Learning to change your mindset, like learning other skills, is a process, not a switch, and doesn't happen overnight.
- Be gentle with yourself when learning new attitudes and skills – you're more likely to stick with the learning!
- Learning is not an overnight process, there are a number of natural stages that we all go through. The moment you begin to increase your awareness is generally the moment your confidence will take a dip. Don't be discouraged – stick with the learning!
- Praise your own efforts.
- Change causes a predictable range of emotions often in a more or less predictable sequence – 'forewarned is forearmed'.

More information

Godin, S (2007) *The Dip: The extraordinary benefits of knowing when to quit (and when to stick)*, Piatkus, London

Pink, D H (2008) *A Whole New Mind: Why right-brainers will rule the future*, Marshall Cavendish Business, London

3
Personal responsibility and choice – cutting your own path

I n this chapter I describe the importance of choice. There's a distinction between having options and making choices. Making a choice is a decision, and deciding in favour of one option often means ruling out other options. I'll explore the research as to why it's useful to make decisions that are irreversible. First of all let's consider the breadth of areas in life in which we have choices. I hope that recognizing the full extent of these areas will enable you to become more discerning about where you choose to spend your time, and how you spend both your physical and mental energy.

Circle of control

Stephen Covey in his book, *The Seven Habits of Highly Effective People* (1989), suggests that we are faced with a number of concerns. These might range from our health, our children, and problems at work, might include the banking situation or foreign policy through to animal welfare. Within any range of concerns

FIGURE 3.1   Circle of control

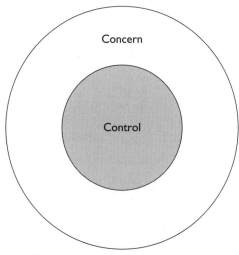

Adapted from Covey, 1989

that we may have, there is always a subset of items over which we have some influence or control (see Figure 3.1).

Take an initial guess: how much time do you currently spend in your (inner) circle of control versus the (outer) circle of concern?

The more time we spend in our circle of control taking action, the more likely it is for the circle to expand. Conversely, the more time we spend in the circle of concern – talking about things but not taking action – the circle of control shrinks. Think about that for a moment: in effect the more you worry, the less control you have.

Think about people that you consider already have great days at work. I expect they are likely to be more proactive, often by asking themselves a simple question: 'What can I do in this situation?' I suspect they have a certain demeanour, and spend more time in their circle of control focusing on what can be done. To have great days at work I recommend you focus your efforts on spending more time in your circle of control.

Focusing on the outer circle of concern can be demoralizing, and not the place you want to spend time if you want great days at work. I've noticed that people, sometimes even quite senior professionals, focus on concerns outside their control and have seemingly naïve expectations of the organization. In doing so, they relinquish their agency and drive. If you find yourself in this camp in any aspect of your life, it's worth taking a deeper look to understand the negative impact that it can have. Perhaps all you are aware of is that you are a bit 'down' and you've never really realized why or how it happens, in which case the following section may shed some light!

There are two main downsides to operating outside your circle of control. It's demoralizing and leads to reduced performance.

Demoralizing

Spending time and energy in the outer circle of concern can become demoralizing as it's an area where we are unlikely to effect change. In a business environment I've noticed that sometimes people seem unable to take ownership of problems, appearing to prefer to mildly complain about 'stuff', or exhibit an expectation that someone else is responsible.

I'm not saying that it's wrong to moan or complain; after all there can be some group camaraderie in negative emotions (Graham *et al*, 2008). Indeed sometimes it's important to get stuff off your chest so that you can move on to something more productive. However, I do suggest you limit the amount of time and energy you spend. Moaning about 'the system' or that it's 'someone else's problem' can become an unhealthy habit. A habit is something that's done without thought – and not a habit that you want if you want more great days at work.

Why? Negative moods can be contagious, and if you want more great days at work then you probably don't want to continually surround yourself with people who accept your moaning. How do I know that they accept your moaning? It's because the unwritten, unspoken, implicit agreement between you and your colleagues is that they accept your moans and, in turn, you accept their moans and complaints. This complicity is no big problem in itself until you analyse how much time you might be spending mired in this swamp of negativity. When you are in that state you are not making progress and as we shall see later the negative emotions are taking a physical toll on your body and health.

You've perhaps heard the expression 'a bad workman blames his tools', and you may know of people who don't take responsibility. An individual believes that he or she gives a rationale (read excuse) for something not happening on a case-by-case basis, giving a different excuse for each situation. However, others tend to notice the broader patterns of behaviour. People begin to notice that 'she always has an excuse', which can be poisonous to your career and relationships, and success becomes more elusive, destined always to happen to someone else.

Conversely, some people attribute all the blame to themselves, and never to the situation or lack of actions by others. As you critically evaluate your behaviour when it comes to taking ownership, you may find this chapter will be of use to you too.

I'm not suggesting that you take ownership of *everything* – but as you become more aware of what you are taking ownership for, and what you're not owning, you can start to take some different choices. Ironically, taking ownership for what you can change is liberating, giving you more influence rather than becoming a trap. The more you take ownership of things that you can change, the more influential you become – which starts a more virtuous circle.

Reduced performance

Often when people operate in the outer circle of concern, their language is full of moans, whinges and blame. When operating outside of the circle of control, it's 'someone else's problem', whether it's the government, the organization, the boss, the other department ... Perhaps a shrug of the shoulders and phrases such as 'it's not me guv'nor!', or 'the computer says no'. There may be reasons not to take ownership – and perhaps there are systems in place that it's not appropriate to circumnavigate. However, playing the blame game takes energy.

In many business environments people seek to avoid blame. As I think about two individuals 'defending their corner' and trying not to be shouldered with the blame, my mind's eye pictures two children playing 'tag': the energetic dance to catch and tap the other player to say 'tag, you're it', and then to sidestep quickly the person now 'it'. Whilst this is a fun and energetic game for children, it's not so useful in the business environment – especially given the research on high-performing teams (Fredrickson and Losada, 2005) which shows that higher-performance teams that asked questions as much as they defended their own views and cast their attention outward as much as inward had higher connectivity to one another. (See Chapter 11 for more information.)

In business, when people are focused on finding different ways to allocate or avoid blame, during that instant the work that people are being paid to do is not getting done. Perhaps the individual catches up on the work by rushing it through at the end of the day, or perhaps it gets left undone or done badly. Whilst a single element of pondering on a concern will not knock an individual's overall performance or effectiveness, the more it becomes a habit the worse it becomes.

My boss will look out for me

Historically many organizations were paternalistic, 'taking good care' of employees, many of whom had a 'job for life'. Perhaps this encouraged learned helplessness (Hiroto and Seligman, 1975), and a 'don't rock the boat' attitude within the organization. However, within many organizations times have changed; they want more pro-activeness, more active choices by the employee.

I have seen quite senior professionals, even in a situation as personal as a career promotion, having a naïve expectation that someone else will take ownership and that they'll receive a promotion without taking any action. I think the thought is, 'If I work hard(er) I will get noticed and receive a promotion for my good work'. And yes, sometimes this does happen. However, more and more this is not the case. Even when leaders initiate development conversations, there can be an almost child-like expectation that 'the boss should know best what's available and what my skills are'. Although there's truth in the statement, a manager may have a broader view of the roles available within the organization; however, it's also useful as a manager to have some awareness of what type of role the individual wants – which is where a proactive approach is required.

Bring concerns into your circle of control

Increasingly employees are being encouraged to take more initiative and responsibility, especially for their own careers. Peterson (2006) describes an authoritative leadership style which 'entails limits with explanations and on-going negotiations ... which leads to employees who are independent yet responsible'. To encourage what's described as internal locus of control with individuals, managers and leaders within organizations have to ensure that employees have some control, otherwise there is a risk of wasting energy defending blame or learned helplessness.

This is an issue across hierarchies within organizations; even some senior executives often do not have a clear understanding of what they can do to bring concerns into their circle of control. This is a 'life skill' that needs to be learned by all and doesn't just come with promotion.

I've found the work of Covey and his circle of influence a great way to remind people of their *agency*, that is their ability to take action. If you choose, you can take action ... asking yourself the question 'what can I do?' starts to focus you on what can be done, ie *conceptualizing the goal* rather than talking about the problem, which is in and of itself empowering. This is supported by the research on hope, described on page 53.

Mustering determination

Nothing in this world can take the place of persistence. Talent will not; nothing is more common than unsuccessful people with talent. Genius will not; unrewarded genius is almost a proverb. Education will not; the world is full of educated derelicts. Persistence and determination alone are omnipotent. The slogan 'press on' has solved and always will solve the problems of the human race.

Calvin Coolidge

Technically this section should be called 'hope'. However, as a layperson I would previously have described the concept of hope as allied to 'wishful thinking', which it is not. I found the scientific definition of 'hope' surprising (Lopez *et al*, 2004):

Hope reflects individuals' perceptions of their capacities to (1) clearly conceptualize goals; (2) develop the specific strategies to reach those goals (pathways thinking); and (3) initiate and sustain the motivation for using those strategies (agency thinking).

'Hope' in this context is more about determination than wishful thinking. Whatever the obstacle (within reason), a way can be found to overcome. To me this is also about the growth mindset because in a specific context if a person 'fails' at an obstacle, with a fixed mindset they might give up, whereas with a growth mindset, they're more likely to look for other *pathways* around, through or over the obstacles (more information on the fixed and growth mindset can be found in Chapter 2).

Interpreting Ford's quote 'whether you think you can, or whether you think you can't you're probably right', if you think something's not possible then you're not likely to invest time or energy into defining the goals or pathways to achieve it. If you throw in a fixed mindset, then you are really scuppered. However, with goals, agency, pathways, thinking that you 'can' and perhaps a bit of luck (yes, luck) then it's likely that you'll find ways of making something happen. I'll return to the concept of luck later in the chapter.

Being in control

Research has shown that being in control of one's life is an important factor in health and well-being. I'll briefly describe two important and significant studies.

In the first study, Langer and Rodin (1976) conducted groundbreaking research in nursing homes which demonstrated the importance of taking personal responsibility. In the nursing home, the staff typically took care of everything for the patients. Before making the intervention, the researchers tested patients on two wards on a range of dimensions. For the intervention itself to test the element of control, on one ward patients were given responsibility to look after a small plant. To provide a comparison or control, patients on the other ward weren't given a plant, but they were similar in all other aspects.

In the tests on both groups after the intervention, the plant owners had more positive moods, were more alert and more active. Even more interesting and quite surprising is that the 'plant carers' had 50 per cent fewer deaths than the other group in the course of the next 18 months. I think it's quite phenomenal to think that the simple act of giving patients a plant to look after, which meant that they had something for which they were responsible, seemed to give them a sense of control – which in turn led to a longer life!

This is not the only study with such a finding. Sir Michael Marmot conducted significant research into mortality within Whitehall (Marmot and Smith, 1991). He found those in more senior positions lived longer. Whilst you might be thinking that this could be down to a number of factors, the research controlled mathematically for the effects of income, education and risk factors (such as smoking) on health. Marmot identified as significant 'being in control' of one's life.

The moral of these two examples is that being in control leads to a longer life. The invitation is to take more control and ownership of your life. The research has demonstrated that you'll live longer and have great days at work. You may wonder just how you can take more control of your work/life and that's the next topic.

Choice

The research around choice is not necessarily intuitive, but really worth the effort to understand as it will help you to unlock your future! Over the next few pages I'll cover the following:

- When we make a choice we often **eliminate other options.** This can feel a bit scary and sometimes prevents people from making choices, ie can lead to procrastination.
- **There's a cost to indecision.**
- There's **false intuition** around the span of choice. There are areas in life we think we should have choice over but the research indicates it's not good for our well-being to have too many options. In fact too many options can stall decision making altogether, which is why in sales settings you are often presented with just three. Good, better and best. It is also human nature to choose the middle option.
- **The speed of making the decision** and the inability to revoke the decision counter-intuitively leads to more happiness.

And the following chapters expand further on these aspects of choice:

- Our choices are determined by what's important to us – our values (Chapter 4).
- There are areas of our life we probably didn't know we have choice over, but yet we do. These aspects have significant impact on our well-being and therefore can be hugely influential in increasing our experience of having great days at work, for example our perspective of time and our emotions – which will be covered more fully in Chapters 5 and 6.

Eliminate other options

Options are decisions that we haven't yet committed to. Many of us from an early age were encouraged to keep our options open – not to reduce our (future career) options too soon. Unfortunately the very advice given to help increase the likelihood of success may in fact hold us back at a later stage. Coyle suggests that even for young people, making a choice at a young age can lead to exceptional performance – which is counter to popular myths of keeping options open (Coyle, 2009).

We live in a time of many choices and options, and research (Verme, 2009) describes, 'A variable that measures freedom of choice and the locus of control is found to predict life satisfaction better than any other known factor ...'. However, there is also considerable research suggesting that keeping our options open is detrimental to both making progress and our happiness.

Decision making takes energy, no matter the size of the decision. At some point we have to make a choice: decide. As a result of the choices that we make about what 'to do', it also affects what we're not going to do. On a restaurant menu, in the past choosing one dish meant excluding the other choices. Of course with the advent of tasting menus we don't have to exclude items from the menu, we can sample everything! Perhaps it's a societal theme of wanting it all. People can get a bit knotted with the dilemma of wanting to keep their options open whilst making a decision. This inner turmoil can lead to procrastination. Constantly revisiting decisions is unproductive; it drains energy which could be used to have great days at work. First let's look at our instinctive desire to keep options open.

The cost of keeping our options open

The 'cost' of indecision has been researched by behavioural psychologist Dan Ariely (2008). His team developed a computer program that showed three different coloured doors. Within the program, by clicking on a coloured door participants in the experiment could enter a room of the same colour.

Once in a room each subsequent click of the mouse would earn a small amount of money (between 1 and 10 cents), and each room had a different earning range. For example, the red room might range from 2 to 4 cents per click, whilst the blue room had monetary amounts from 4 to 6 cents, and the green room, 5 to 7 cents. The objective was to get the most money, which involved finding the room with the biggest payoff and clicking on it as many times as possible. The computer kept a running tally of the amount. In the initial experiment participants just had to find the room with the biggest payout and click in the room for the duration of the experiment (100 clicks) to earn the most points.

A devious twist happened in a follow-up experiment. Any door left unvisited for 12 clicks would disappear. There was a visual indicator showing how close to disappearing each door was. In this experiment participants were in a frenzy to keep the doors open – clicking between the rooms (and using clicks from the quota) to stop the doors disappearing – no matter what the payout. On one hand switching rooms is a good strategy to find the room with the largest payout, but 'burning clicks' to keep the doors of lesser paying rooms open seemed like an odd, but instinctive strategy for participants. Results showed participants instinctively kept their doors open by dashing between rooms and 'burning clicks' as a result (Isen, 2009). They typically made 15 per cent less money than those in the first experiment. Ariely suggests: 'The truth is that they could have made more money by picking a room – any room – and merely staying there for the whole experiment!'

The false intuition of decision making

Before I set out on the research for this book I thought that having great days at work would involve 'choice' in decisions. Perhaps this is because I remember occasions in my career where I've been 'told' to do something, and I didn't feel any choice in the situation. I felt quite miffed at the lack of autonomy. Certainly at first glance Verme's research seems to support the view that we're better off having freedom of choice and given the research I mentioned earlier from

Langer and Rodin, and Marmot on the importance of control in situations, I thought choice would have been important. But as Ariely's research show, although we intuitively 'keep our options open' this does not support us in developing our well-being as you'll see next.

Become master of the speedy decision

I remember a senior executive within IBM describing how to present to executives. He defined the role of the presenter as providing and presenting the relevant information in order for the decision to be made. The specific examples were around whether a particular IT project, with the investment of time and money, should be supported. The role of the recipients, in this case the executives, was to make a fast decision, allowing the energy and enthusiasm of the team either to flow into the resultant action or to be directed elsewhere, rather than being stalled by 'no decision'.

What the IBM executive was encouraging (fast decision making) is supported by research from Dan Gilbert (2002). In one experiment two groups of volunteers had attended a short photography course. During the course they had taken 12 photographs of things meaningful to them and then invested six hours of their time learning how to use a dark room and subsequently developing two of their favourite pictures into large glossy prints. At the end of the course they were (unexpectedly) told they had to give one of the pictures up as some sort of 'proof of attendance', and they wouldn't see the print again; they had to choose which print they wanted to keep.

The first group of volunteers were asked to make a final, unchanging decision to choose which of the two photos they wanted to keep (an irreversible decision). The second group were also told to make a decision, but they could change their mind as to which photo to submit within the next four days (a reversible decision).

Having made their (initial) decision as to which photo to keep, in the next part of the experiment, the volunteers were then randomly assigned to either the role of 'forecaster' or 'experiencer'. In the experiencer role they simply had to rate how much they liked the photo they kept.

In the role of the forecaster they were asked to predict which group of volunteers would like the photo they kept more: the group that had to make the fast and irreversible decision, or the group that had the weekend to reverse the decision and change their minds.

Take a moment to put yourself in the forecaster role. How much difference do you think the speed of making the decision would make to the 'liking satisfaction' of the picture they kept?

The forecasters suggested that there wouldn't be much in it, perhaps marginally more satisfaction from those who made the irreversible decision.

The findings showed that: 'contrary to forecasters' predictions, those experiencers who had been given the opportunity to change their outcome were **less likely** to grow relatively fond of it over the course of several days than were the experiencers who had not been given that opportunity' (Gilbert, 2002).

Although we like to think choice makes us happier and more satisfied with our decisions, the research shows that when *stuck* with a choice they have made, people become much more satisfied.

In another similar experiment, a fresh set of volunteers were to decide to which of the experimental groups (unchangeable or changeable) they wished to be assigned. Results showed that participants *preferred to be assigned* to the group where they had longer to decide which photo to submit. However, the research showed this group were the *least satisfied* with their picture. Findings such as these demonstrate how poor we are at predicting our own happiness.

Common to both studies above was an element of choice. Initially, I understood that Gilbert's research suggested that having *choice* was not good for well-being. However, I think it's more related to the speed of making (irreversible) decisions. Each group of volunteers had a choice as to which of their artworks to keep – but the satisfaction came with a fast, irreversible decision. Take a moment to consider what this information means for you. Gather information, make a decision and move on. The longer you take to make a decision, ultimately the less satisfied you're likely to be.

I confess I was slightly disappointed by these findings, since I had always liked the ability to be flexible and spontaneous. However, counter intuitively it seems that we're happier with our choices if they have to be made quickly, and then, once the decision has been made, it becomes irreversible.

'Positive' feelings associated with making an irreversible decision, in more extreme circumstances, come from Frankl, a holocaust survivor (Frankl, 2004). In describing a particular decision not to try to escape he said: 'I ran out of the hut and told my friend I couldn't go with him. As soon as I told him with finality that I had made up my mind to stay with my patients, the unhappy feeling left me'.

Make a decision, move on

Decisions lead to action; actions maintain momentum. Conversely lack of decisiveness can lead to stagnation, procrastination and ultimately fear and powerlessness. Chapter 8 describes two different decision-making strategies, those of satisficing (the good enough decision) and maximizing (thorough research before committing to a decision). It seems that a satisficing decision leads to more happiness. It might be counter intuitive for many of us, but make the decision and move on!

What if the decision is not ours to make

It can be frustrating to be seemingly at the whim of someone else. One thing you can do in such a situation is to ask yourself some questions: 'What can I do to move this forward?' or 'Who else needs to be involved?' Often there's not a single 'right way'; there are multiple ways. One chief operating officer I worked with described how people would constantly interrupt work looking for a quick purchasing decision: 'Sure it only takes a second to say yes or no to the request, but what most professionals don't do is present me with the relevant information in context.' So if you're the professional wanting a decision from someone else then be proactive and find what additional information the decision maker will need, and present it in a useful way.

When working with acquisition companies one decision which is outside of most people's control is whether the offices will be relocated. This raises a myriad of questions from professionals. What will the new commute be like? Will there be parking? Will I have to pay for coffee? Will I be able to bring my dog to the new offices? One thing I've noticed is that, rather than asking the questions, often people catastrophize, jumping quickly to the worst case scenario. Decisions do have to be thought through, and the relevant facts gathered, and this can take time. Ask the questions; be sure not to jump to catastrophization (covered more in Chapter 5).

Group decisions

Gaining full consensus and agreement can be popular forms of decision making in some industries and in some cultures. There's a risk that decisions taken by committee result in mediocre decisions because they are 'average' decisions and provide the path of least resistance. This can be fine, but it can also be useful to think about the context of the decision to see whether a more 'risky' or perhaps 'bold' decision could be usefully taken.

Involving more people often slows the decision process down. Ensuring that the decision makers have appropriate relevant information to make a decision is useful. However, sometimes opinion gets confused with factual information. Take an example of upgrading the office IT. Which technology solution is best for the office? Typically there is no one 'right way', different technologies will have strengths and weaknesses and different people will have their opinions on the relative priorities of different attributes of the system. When making decisions in groups, it can be useful to have a clear set of criteria at the outset.

I was involved in the recruitment of graduates for many years. There was a clear set of criteria which everyone involved in the decision was trained to use, so that when the time came to make what can be an emotive decision as to which candidates to employ – everyone was clearly focused on the criteria.

Money-back guarantee

Whilst shops may offer you a 30-day exchange policy, it seems in life we're better off making 'non-returnable' decisions. Having the ability to revoke our decision doesn't make us any happier with our choice, and in fact it might make us unhappier. As you're developing your ability to have great days at work you may want to test making faster irrevocable decisions and notice the impact on you, your energy and well-being.

Did you know you have choice over this...

In the material world of buying products and goods it seems that choice is not good for our well-being. In *The Paradox of Choice* (2004) Barry Schwartz describes the overwhelming choice for denim jeans, but rather than this adding to his well-being he's left wondering (briefly) about whether he's opted for the most flattering style and colour. What I'm going to say next can be anathema to many. I'll try and present it in a soft way. To a large extent you can choose your emotions, and this can have a positive impact on your well-being.

This can be accomplished by deliberately choosing how you focus, and what you focus on rather than 'drifting', waiting for a tide or current to take you in a particular direction. I recognize that sometimes our habits can be so outside our awareness, and so automatic that they don't always seem like choices. I'll try and be gentle and I'd encourage you to be gentle with yourself too. As you start to put any new skills into practice, it's unlikely that you'll achieve mastery within 24 hours! I'll return to emotions in Chapter 6. For now I'll continue to explore the concept of choice and focus.

Look at Figure 3.2. What do you see?

A white vase, or two faces looking at each other? Both are there. I think the same is often true in life: we can notice the good or the

FIGURE 3.2   The white vase

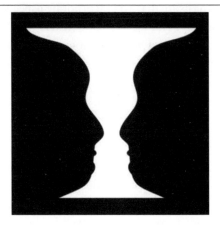

bad, it's a choice. I realize that at the moment it may not feel like a choice. Where we choose to focus our attention and energy is of great importance to our quality of life and ultimately our health.

Take a moment to think about what you've typically been focused on. Is your *modus operandi* 'head down battling to work', or strolling along with time to smell the spring blossom (or depending on the season: feel the warmth of the sun on your back; enjoy the crunch of the autumn leaves; or the sparkle of frost on cobwebs)? Do you remember the good or fret over the bad? Neither is right or wrong; however, it is likely that you'll have a very different emotional response depending on which you 'choose'.

I first came across the expression 'you get what you focus on' when I took my advanced driving test. My instructor, an ex-police officer, told me if ever I found myself in a skid, to focus on the *gap* between any objects, rather than the object, whether it be a telegraph pole, a tree or a parked car. He noted that many accidents happen on virtually clear stretches of road, where the car hits the only object for miles, *because* it becomes the object of our focus.

I think the adage 'you get what you focus on' is very powerful, and you may want to ensure that you incorporate aspects of your whole life so that you don't end up like King Midas. You may remember that King Midas, from Greek mythology, asked for everything he touched to turn to gold. He was granted his wish ... but sadly as he had not thought through the implications fully, his wife and daughter turned to gold as he touched them, and ultimately he starved to death as his food turned to gold before he could eat it.

In a similar way you probably wouldn't want success at work at the expense of your relationships – and if by some small chance sacrificing relationships on the road to 'success' sounds appealing, then I feel I should point out that the importance of social connections has been noted in many studies on well-being. I'll be describing some of those studies in Chapter 10.

Optimism or pessimism

There's a debate in academia about whether optimism, pessimism or realism leads to better health and well-being. Terms such as 'dispositional optimism', 'defensive pessimism' and 'flexible or complex optimism' are bandied around – I think academia likes jargon more than those of us in business!

Despite these learned terms and much research it seems that studies have reached different conclusions. The research shows that they each have their merits. Which I think is good news. It's not our approach, it's how we use it! I think the approach of expecting the best but planning for alternatives is useful.

Often people who describe themselves as optimists describe themselves as lucky, so I thought it would be useful in the context of having great days at work to explore the research on luck.

Luck

Professor Wiseman (2003) demonstrated that people make their own luck. This may sound hard to believe so I'll describe the research. Wiseman designed an experiment which asked participants to count the number of photos in a newspaper, and the response would be timed. In the newspaper – which he'd specifically created – he had also put in letters '2 inches high' the words 'stop counting – there are 43 photographs'. Some people – those that described themselves as unlucky – missed or ignored those words as they were too busy focusing on the original task of counting the photographs. Those that described themselves as lucky noticed the information – and therefore finished the task more quickly.

Based on Wiseman's experiment it seems that our disposition towards luck can affect our reality – when we think we're lucky we spot more opportunities. Actually, it seems that we create more opportunities by changing daily routines, doing different things and meeting new people. Wiseman also suggests that if you experience something bad, imagine how it could have been worse, so be lucky and expect good things to happen. In order to have great days at work, occasionally take a different route to work, find ways to meet different people – and stay focused on being lucky – and who knows what good things will happen!

You get what you focus on ... so why not focus on having fun, smiling at people, and expecting good things to happen.

Summary

- Focus on what's in your control as operating outside your circle of control is demoralizing and generally ineffective.
- To bring something into your circle of control ask yourself, 'What can I do?'
- Be determined to find ways round obstacles.
- Being in control is an important factor in health and well-being.
- Making a choice eliminates other options.
- We think we should have more choice – but when we're 'stuck' with something we're generally happier.

- There is a cost to indecision. Whilst evaluating alternative options no choice has being taken.
- We intuitively want to keep our options open – but this prevents us from making progress.
- We do have choice over our emotions (covered more fully in Chapter 6).
- Act lucky, be lucky. Break with daily routines to create chance opportunities and deal with bad luck by thinking how the situation could have been worse.

More information

In the context of how we make errors in predicting what makes us happy, you might be interested in investing 20 minutes to watch Dan Gilbert's (2004) TED webcast: **http://www.youtube.com/watch?v=LTO_dZUvbJA.**

Part Two
CREATE
A BETTER FUTURE

4
Vision – the first step in bringing your desired future into reality

If you don't know where you are going, any road will get you there.

Adapted from Lewis Carroll

Dan Ariely (2008) is a behavioural economist interested in our decision-making processes. One area of particular interest is when we behave in a 'predictably irrational' way in our choices. Sometimes any decision is better than no decision – and yet we procrastinate. Ariely illustrates the predictably irrational choice of procrastination with a story of a donkey approaching a barn.

In brief, the story goes that at each end of the barn is a bale of hay. The donkey approaches the barn, stops and looks from one to the other of the two bales. The donkey is undecided as to which bale might best suit his hunger. Sadly the donkey dies of starvation whilst making the decision. Now I'm not suggesting that you will starve if you don't have a vision or a direction, but I am suggesting that life will be easier if you know what's important to you, and you have a long-term vision.[1]

FIGURE 4.1   Inputs to your vision

There are two aspects to this chapter. Firstly, I describe why having *your own vision* of how you want to live your life is so important. Essentially it's because a personal vision connects you to your own source of motivation. This internal or intrinsic motivation (described more fully later in the chapter) has been demonstrated to be a powerhouse of energy.

Secondly, I'll encourage you to get practical with a couple of activities to assist you to find or refine your vision and motivation, because for so many people purpose and passion (the result of having vision) leads to having great days at work. There can be many inputs to finding your vision so if you don't find it at the first pass, no worries; it is for many people an iterative process with many inputs (see Figure 4.1).

If you don't know what would make a great day at work, how can you achieve it? Whilst the conversation around the coffee machine might be answering the question, 'What would you do if you won the lottery?', given that the odds of winning the UK jackpot are 1 in approximately 14 million, can we begin to fulfil at least some of those dreams in another way? Would our energy be better spent taking action towards our dreams rather than just idly fantasizing about spending our winnings?

Why set long-range goals when who knows what's round the corner?

Having a long-term vision gives you a broad focus for your day-to-day choices, decision making and actions. The motivational aspect of having a broad vision or distal goals is supported by research (Grant, 2006).

Sometimes it can be easier to focus on the long term, and think about what *you* want to achieve. This can release you from other people's (more immediate) expectations of you. Some people have a clear vision of how they want to live their lives and their long-range goals. However, many of the people I've coached and trained don't have such a clear vision.

There are many reasons for not having a vision: sometimes people have never thought about it, just taking one life event at a time; others don't want to be disappointed if life doesn't work out the way they anticipate. In the words of Spike Milligan: 'We have no plans, therefore nothing can go wrong.'

I've coached people who have achieved their work-related goals. If they're not fully aware of having achieved their goals, or they don't have 'the next goal' in mind, I've noticed that they then wonder why they feel a bit 'flat' and uninspired.

I've also coached people who wanted to remain open to external opportunities. The downside has been that their career became stuck – not wanting to give themselves a direction for fear it would be the 'wrong' one, and waiting for the right opportunity to 'present itself'. Typically, as soon as they set themselves a vision, their motivation kicks in, or perhaps actions follow and then motivation kicks in – either way people have found it contributes to having great days at work.

What does the research say

Grant noted that studies have shown that the effects of goal setting can be long lasting. For example, managers' goals for the number of levels of future promotion have been found to be a significant predictor of the number of promotions received over a 25-year time span (Grant, 2006).

Lyubomirsky (2010) described it more broadly:

> People who strive for something personally significant, whether it's learning a new craft, changing careers or raising moral children, are far happier than those who don't have strong dreams or aspirations. Find a happy person and you will find a project.

What are you striving for?

I think if you've got some goals in mind, it will be easier to get value from the rest of the chapter. Plus the process of setting your vision often involves iteration and refinement. So, to get you started I've chosen a quick (5–10 minutes) and effective goal-setting activity. It's based on a workshop from Ian Stewart, co-author of *TA Today* (Stewart and Joines, 1987) and co-founder of The Berne Institute of Psychotherapy, which in turn is his adaptation of the work of Alan Lakein, best-selling author on personal time management.

ACTIVITY   Goals part I

This activity should take no more than about five minutes. You will need a sheet of paper (I suggest A4 or larger), a pencil or pen and a timer. There are no 'right' answers – this is about discovering your goals. The purpose of this exercise is to help you identify and clarify what *you* want. There are a couple of variations – read through and pick which *one* you want to do.

Write at the top of the sheet of paper: **What are my lifetime goals**?

Start timing. Take exactly **two minutes** to write down your answers to that question. Write as much as comes to mind – don't attempt to censor or evaluate. Put down everything you bring to mind within the allotted two minutes.

Many people find looking at a blank page a bit daunting; if this is you, you might prefer one of the variations below.

Variation 1: You may find it helps if you start by identifying the main areas of your life in which you may have goals you want to satisfy. Possible areas might be, for example: job; health; relationships; leisure; family; or whatever other areas are most important to you.

Variation 2: This activity will take slightly longer – a total of six minutes. Take 60 seconds per question to brainstorm the answers to each of the following (Rohn, 1985):

● What do you want to do?
● What do you want to become?
● What do you want to see?
● What do you want to have?
● Where do you want to go?
● What do you want to share?

Whichever variation you choose, when you have completed the brainstorm, take another two minutes to review what you have written. Alter or add to it in any way which you feel makes the list more satisfying to you.

Whatever you've put on paper, you've made a great start in developing your goals. Remember, often people spend more time planning their summer holiday than they do their life. If this is one of the first times for a while that you've done any long-range thinking then you may not be entirely comfortable with the results. Don't worry! As we go through the rest of the chapter there are additional activities designed to support you in taking your thoughts and working with you to mould them into a form that you find compelling.

Visualization

Many self-help books encourage the use of visualization, typically encouraging you to imagine you have achieved everything you ever wanted, to luxuriate in the feelings of success and so on. There is much research supporting the notion that when hypothetical events are imagined, people are more likely to believe that the event will occur.

It's not just belief that the events will occur. By way of 'proof', there's an interesting study that demonstrates that people are more likely to purchase cable TV if they have visualized owning it first (Gregory *et al*, 1982). So there is some scientific research supporting visualization; however, there's more research suggesting that the way visualization is carried out is important.

Not all visualization leads to results

While doing some research on different ways of visualizing, I discovered a couple of really important pieces of research which can dramatically increase the effectiveness of your visualization.

Firstly a study (Taylor *et al*, 1998) in which a goal had been set for all participants. One group of participants visualized having achieved the goal – ie focusing solely on the 'outcome'. The second group visualized what they needed to do in order to achieve the goal, they visualized the obstacles and how they would overcome them. The researchers described this as visualizing the 'process'.

The research found that the value of visualization comes from anticipating problems and being able to handle them (ie those participants in 'the process' group achieved higher levels of success in reaching their goal). Indeed those that only visualized the outcome achieved lower scores.

A second study by Kappes and Oettingen (2011) suggests that visualizations that idealize the future are found to be inversely related to achievement over time. They found that the more positively the fantasies are experienced, the less effort people invest in the actual achievement.

I think there are two important points. Firstly, I suggest that one important aspect to visualization is that it 'forces' one to have a goal or an outcome in mind. With that outcome in mind, when visualizing, be sure to anticipate the steps one needs to go through in order to achieve your goal.

So like the athlete who visualizes winning gold, she's not just visualizing the feeling of running over the finishing line, she's imagining her perfect race, from the starting blocks, step by step. Remember: the visualization is based on your goals, which will include things which are within your control.

TIP

Visualize both the goal and the steps needed to achieve your goal, along with how you will overcome obstacles.

Without long-range vision, sometimes we can become too focused

To see how good your focus (attention) is follow the link below; it's quick, less than two minutes, simple and confidential, and will give you a great starting point for the rest of this chapter. It's an online test from Chabris and Simons so go ahead and type in the URL: **http://wn.com/selective_attention_test**.

The downside of focused attention

For some, the results of the selective attention test referred to above may be surprising. It can be hard to believe that when our attention is too focused on something we utterly miss what we're not paying attention to. This is very similar to the research in the previous chapter about luck, and missing the message which took up half the page in letters two inches high. So why does this happen? Wiseman (2003) has found that anxiety disrupts people's ability to notice the unexpected. Many of us have busy lives, and whilst we're busy focusing on 'the next thing', whether it's meeting that looming project deadline, collecting the kids from school or even what to pick up from the supermarket for dinner, we can fail to see things which may translate into missing opportunities.

Having a long-range vision can keep things in perspective, and ensure that some of the short-term activities don't distract us from our bigger vision.

One of the things I've noticed is that people are typically very good at stating what they don't want in a situation: 'Anything but this!' Having a vision creates a clear direction that you do want, and it seems that knowing what we want primes our subconscious to look for it.

A note on language

You may have seen the books which implore you to think yourself rich, or thinner ... and you may have thought 'rubbish', or words to that effect. However, there is *something* about being deliberately focused on what you do want, prioritizing it and working towards it rather than being focused on what you don't want, or what you want to stop doing. Focus is different to wishing; it involves taking action. Being focused on hitting your sales target can be taken positively: 'What action can I take today that will move me towards that result?'; or 'I can sit and worry and say I'm NEVER going to hit my target.' By focusing on the negative your reduce the likelihood of taking action, along with finding all the supporting reasons why you will not hit your target.

> Teaser.
>
> If I say to you: 'Whatever you do next, don't think of a blue donkey', what happens?

It seems that the brain doesn't easily process 'nots' and 'don'ts' – and if I tell you, 'Don't think of a blue donkey', for many of us the image of a blue donkey first comes into our heads before being erased or over-written in some way. For a phrase stated in the 'negative' the brain has to create different, sometimes random, links and you're not reinforcing what you *do* want:

- Because the brain momentarily filters the 'don't', for a fraction of a moment the brain is focused exactly on what's not wanted. Often this is where the processing of the statement stops.

- However, sometimes alternatives options are created ... If not the blue donkey – then what? A white elephant? A pink giraffe?

- There can be errors in translation – just because you don't want to think of a blue donkey it doesn't necessarily follow that you want to think of a pink giraffe.

Let's take an example of the phrase: 'I ~~don't~~ want another stressful day at work.' At a subconscious level the person who says this is saying exactly what they don't want. The deletion of the word 'don't' takes place and the 'translation' then starts to happen... Does *not stressful* mean a productive day or a calm day or something else? It may be that each of the options is not *quite* what's sought. I would term this an 'away from' goal.

Away from

The problem with 'away from' goals is there is no clear direction. For a moment, imagine being on roller-skates, tethered by ropes and being pulled in eight[2] different directions (see Figure 4.2). It's likely that the different forces will balance out and equilibrium will be maintained. You are going nowhere fast.

FIGURE 4.2 'Away from' motivation

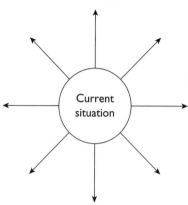

'Away from': energy dispersed

Current situation

Adapted from Hazelton (2012)

So if you find yourself saying you don't want to do your current job, or there's a part of your work that you dislike ... what do you want instead (that you can begin to bring inside your circle of control)?

There is nothing wrong with what I would term an 'away from' goal or an avoidance goal. Indeed these 'away from' situations provide us with energy to do something different, but only when we're focused can we gather our energy and move the situation forward.

It's usually great to harness 'away from' energy with a clear 'towards'. I asked you to think about ropes pulling you in eight different directions – but it's also a metaphor for how your energy is being dissipated.

Towards

Back to the roller-skates. This time imagine all the ropes are intertwined and are pulling you in the same direction. The rope is now eight times as thick. The likelihood is that travel in that direction would be more direct (see Figure 4.3), possibly not even getting stalled by any lumps or bumps in the road! OK, perhaps too far with the metaphor! If you prefer to think about it in terms of energy – when you have a clear vision your energy is focused.

FIGURE 4.3   'Towards' motivation

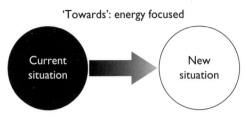

'Towards': energy focused

Adapted from Hazelton (2012)

It is useful to have a clear 'towards' goal. State clearly what you do want. Goal setting and visualization are both approaches to develop your clear 'towards'.

TIP

If you notice yourself saying what you don't want, take a moment to think and be clear about what you want instead. Rephrase it into 'I want' because it will send unambiguous signals to the brain.

The scientific basis for goal setting

In *The Talent Code* (2009), Coyle eloquently describes now, when neurons in the brain fire repeatedly, they develop a sheathing of a substance called myelin. This sheathing or insulation allows the neurons to fire faster. Repeated practice ensures the neurons are sheathed in myelin which acts like a superconductor. Myelination develops when people repeatedly practise doing something.

Having clarity on goals is a similar process. Setting and repeatedly thinking about and actively working towards your goals is a similar process to that which takes place when learning a new skill. New connections are being made, pathways are created and myelin insulation makes them fire faster. This is supported by research from Feltz and Landers (1983, 2007) that shows that while for a motor skill physical practice is superior to mental practice, mental practice produces superior learning compared to no practice at all. It seems that the best method for honing skills and making progress is a combination of both physical and mental practice. To golfers 'the inner game of golf' may be a familiar phrase and tells how important it is to visualize the outcome. Racing car drivers mentally go around the track before a race, playing in their minds how they will prepare and dive through each corner ahead of the actual race. It has been proved that such mental preparation improves accuracy and speed of response.

Priming

I believe the drive to move 'away from' gives energy to change; however, the 'towards', and the repetition of what's wanted, provides priming for the brain to search out what's wanted. The effects of priming are often used in psychology experiments. Dan Ariely (2008) describes experiments asking participants to unscramble sentences which are related to either rudeness or politeness, and then setting up a situation where participants have to interrupt the experimenter. How long the participants would typically wait before they interrupted depended on the types of sentences unscrambled. If participants had unscrambled the sentences on rudeness they interrupted quickly, whereas the participants who unscrambled the sentences on politeness took several minutes to interrupt.

Motivation

Motivation can be said to be the driving force which assists us to achieve our goals. Ultimately motivation is about the initial and on-going spark which fires us to make the first step towards getting things done.

It's interesting to note that when we 'achieve' we tend to feel good, which can often lead to us doing more things, ie achieving becomes self-reinforcing. I've heard a lot of debate over which comes first:

action or motivation. While current research might not be able to answer that directly, it's worth looking at the different qualities of motivation because they affect us in different ways.

Not all motivation is equal

There are many theories about motivation. And indeed a lot has been written about it although it's often written in such a way that suggests motivation is a single concept. There is research (Ryan and Deci, 2001) to support the idea that there are indeed a number of different types of motivation (see Figure 4.4). Understanding that there are different types of motivation gives you the opportunity to find which you find more appealing and start to engineer your life to have more motivating aspects, and hence experience great days at work.

You may be motivated because you enjoy doing something; alternatively you might be motivated because you fear the consequences. Whilst both can be 'motivating' the quality of the motivation might be different. The concept is similar to the *away from* and *towards* goals mentioned previously. Motivation ranges from amotivation, through stages of extrinsic motivation through intrinsic motivation, all of which are described briefly below.

At the left of the chart is **amotivation,** the state of lacking intetion to act (people do not act or act without intent – they just go through the motions). This could be for a number of reasons. For example, the activity is not valued; they don't feel competent to do the activity; or they are not expecting it to yield a desired outcome.

Intrinsic motivation

At the far right of the chart is **intrinsic motivation,** which refers to doing an activity for the inherent satisfaction of the activity itself. Highly autonomous, with lots of benefits. However, much of what adults do is not intrinsically motivated. Figure 4.4 describes different forms of **extrinsic motivation,** and the extent (from left to right) to which the motivations come from the self.

FIGURE 4.4   The self-determination continuum

The self-determination continuum showing types of motivation with their regulatory styles, loci of causality and corresponding processes

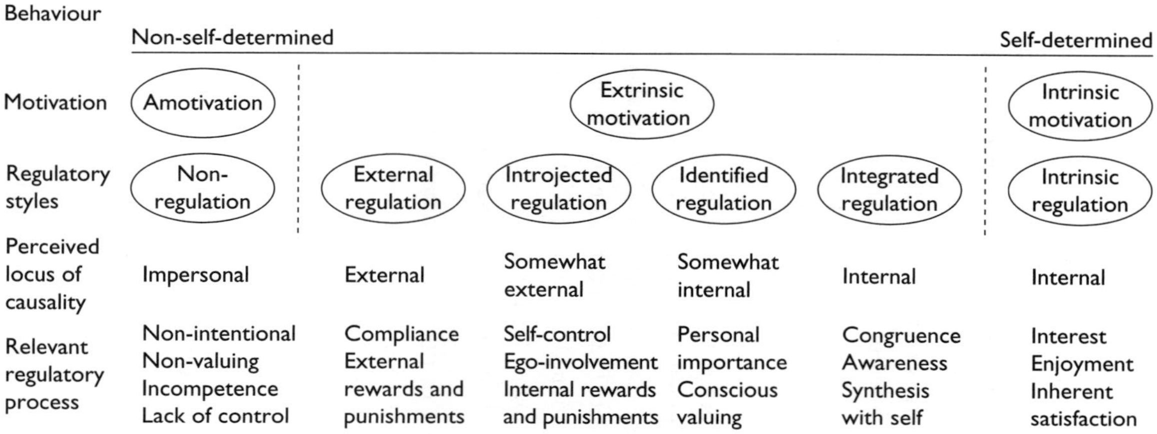

Behaviour	Non-self-determined					Self-determined
Motivation	Amotivation	Extrinsic motivation				Intrinsic motivation
Regulatory styles	Non-regulation	External regulation	Introjected regulation	Identified regulation	Integrated regulation	Intrinsic regulation
Perceived locus of causality	Impersonal	External	Somewhat external	Somewhat internal	Internal	Internal
Relevant regulatory process	Non-intentional Non-valuing Incompetence Lack of control	Compliance External rewards and punishments	Self-control Ego-involvement Internal rewards and punishments	Personal importance Conscious valuing	Congruence Awareness Synthesis with self	Interest Enjoyment Inherent satisfaction

Source: Ryan and Deci, 2000

On the other hand, motivation can come from within and this is called intrinsic motivation. The research shows that there are three elements to intrinsic motivation: autonomy, mastery and purpose.

If you've ever wanted more of any of the following:

- interest;
- excitement;
- confidence;
- enhanced performance;
- persistence;
- creativity;
- heightened vitality;
- self-esteem;
- general well-being;

then the answer is to find your intrinsic motivation. Intrinsic motivation is the tendency 'to seek out novelty and challenges and to extend one's capacities to explore and to learn' (Ryan and Deci, 2000).

Extrinsic motivation

Extrinsic motivation relates to motivation that's external to us. For example, external factors could be in the form of the expectation of a reward or a punishment for something. Indeed just the thought of letting someone down can provide us with the extrinsic motivation to act or do something.

Nuances of motivation

Between 'amotivated' at the far left, and 'intrinsically motivated' on the far right of Figure 4.4, Ryan and Deci describe four flavours of extrinsic motivation, that is, motivation that comes from an external source. The detail behind each is less important than the realization that **not all motivation is the same**. You already know that when you experience motivation, some things feel more like an obligation, whilst others have you excited.

Here's a short description of each. At the left-most is **externally regulated** motivation. This is typically experienced as forced: 'watch the compliance video or else'. Moving towards the right is **introjected regulation** whereby we take actions to avoid guilt, anxiety or as a boost to our ego, but these actions are not really what we want to do.

Further still towards the right is **identified regulation**, whereby we consciously value a behavioural goal, and it has become personally important. The final extrinsic motivation is that of **integrated regulation**, whereby full assimilation has taken place, and there is a congruence with one's other values. Although there are many similarities with intrinsic motivation, they are done to attain a separate outcome.

Daniel Pink, the author of *Drive* (2009), has posted what I think is a phenomenal 10-minute YouTube animation about the research findings around motivation (see page 97). There's also a 20-minute video available of him presenting his findings at TED talks which is also very interesting. The main point he makes is that when it comes to those of us who are paid to use our brains rather than brawn at work, essentially 'carrot and stick' doesn't work. What motivates us is whether we're connected to our purpose.

Therefore, in order to have great days at work you will benefit from knowing what your purpose in life is, and find ways to work towards it. This book will provide you with ways to do exactly that based on proven research.

Early in my career as a new manager, I was responsible for a group of about 40 professionals. We worked remotely from each other, coming together about once per quarter to share learning, discuss new opportunities, network and build what is often called 'community'. Typically, at the end of the business meeting we'd have a social event, where we'd go out together. I disliked organizing the 'social'. However, at the time I had a view that I wouldn't ask anyone else to do what I didn't like or want to do myself.

I remember one of the team approached me, and asked if he could run the next social. I was surprised, thinking, 'Who would want to do that?' However, I realized that it fitted in with his goal of moving from a technical role to a project management role. It was the first step in finding a role that fitted his purpose and it was something he wanted to do.

The lesson I learned was that different things motivate us.

You're not a clone

You are unique, and what truly motivates you, and what your goals are, are likely to be different from those of other people. You are likely to have a different sub-set of interests and strengths, and you are likely to enjoy things that others do not, and *vice versa*. Because of this, there's room for us all to find our niche and to be successful in our own way. This is great news because in order to be successful you 'only' have to tap into your own source of motivation which is a sustainable source of energy.[3] In order to tap into that energy you need to know more about yourself and what you want.

Finding your passion may sound easy (or weird), and I know that many people have become a little numb to their passion or purpose, which can happen for a number of reasons. Let's not focus on the reasons why this happens, but understand that the key to great days at work is to begin to unlock your purpose, and the first step is to *start to notice*:

- What do you do that you enjoy?
- What do you do so that time passes both in an instant and yet lingers?
- If you knew you'd be doing 'this thing' tomorrow then would you bounce out of bed?

Answering these questions is not a one-off activity. You may find it useful to informally record your thoughts in a notebook or journal, and then little by little redesign your life so that it has more purpose. Remember it's your life – you can design it how you want it – and it may not be what others 'think you should do'.

I remember when I finally decided to leave a technical/managerial role to move into training and development: it was not a decision I took lightly. Over the course of a couple of years I had reached the conclusion that developing others was something that I was passionate about and wanted to pursue as a career. I'd been a manager and realized that I enjoyed the coaching aspect. I'd personally invested in training to become a trainer, and I'd run a couple of training courses but the move to a full-time training and development role was a significant step.

Many of my colleagues, mentors and managers thought I was making a poor career choice, and cautioned me against moving into a 'dead-end' role. But when I considered my passion, I knew that developing others was something that I was passionate about, and I've never once regretted the move.

There are many people who are likely to be very interested in *your* motivation, possibly even more interested in it than you are. For example, managers and leaders are interested to motivate you to 'do' something (more). Healthcare professions involve mobilizing others to act in different ways (for example, to change eating, drinking and smoking habits). There's a whole (sales and marketing) industry out there composed of people who are interested in finding out what motivates you to buy something, and to influence you to change your purchasing habits (Ryan and Deci, 2000). Dan Ariely (2008) describes some of the research from behavioural economists and how buying motivation can be manipulated with the enticement of FREE!

Unless you have some direction and purpose, it's likely that you'll bob around on the sea of life. Perhaps you'll get lucky with a current or tide, but it's likely that you'll be blown all around. Like a sailing boat with extended sails, you can harness these external forces – but only if you set your course, and extend your sails. If you do not set your own course you will not find what truly excites and fulfils you.

Finding what you really want

The following activities are designed to encourage you to think about what motivates you, in order to begin to connect you to your intrinsic motivation.

FIGURE 4.5   Inputs to creating a vision

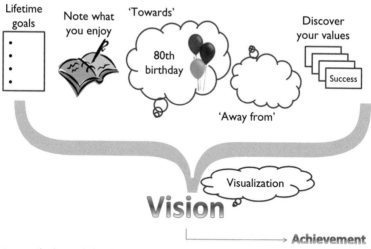

Source: Charlesworth (2013)

Not all people or jobs are the same. Take the role of a librarian. We all think we know what's involved, but the environment can change the role. A librarian in an academic establishment is likely to have a slightly different set of skills and interests than a librarian who drives a mobile library van around villages. So whatever your skills, consider whether using them in a different environment might be more motivating.

If you're continually trying to be something that you're not it's likely to be draining and ultimately unsatisfying.

One vet I know withered in a quiet practice. However, by changing to a new role in a busy emergency out-of-hours clinic, she is positively thriving.

Figure 4.5 represents a selection of inputs into finding your vision. Starting from the left, *lifetime goals* and *note what you enjoy* have already been covered. What follows are two activities where you project yourself into the future and look back. The first is a positive projection designed to give you a *towards* motivation, the second is an *away from*. Finally there's an activity to *discover your values* – the underlying criteria by which you make important decisions.

Each activity will provide input into understanding what's important to you, developing your vision for your future, and thus connecting to your intrinsic motivation. Of course that's just the beginning. Whilst visualizing the steps required to achieve your vision helps, typically people find it useful to develop goals or milestones so they can celebrate achievements along the way. Elbow grease will be required – but of course because it's your vision the 'work' towards it will feel different.

Project forward, look back

It was Stephen Covey, author of *The Seven Habits of Highly Effective People* (1989), who suggested that we 'start with the end in mind'. This is about thinking about mentally transporting yourself to the future, and looking back at some of your key life events and achievements. This will start to uncover what's important to *you*.

There are different ways to do this activity; each variation has a different nuance. The first activity is about developing a *towards* vision. I've plumped for recommending the 80th birthday celebration because I can't see any research suggesting the others are any more effective; it's one I've used extensively and seems to be effective for the majority of people.

ACTIVITY 80th birthday party

Imagine for a moment you're celebrating your 80th birthday, perhaps there are people attending from your former career, as well as your friends, family. They're giving speeches about you and your life's work. Indulge your senses for a moment. Who's there to celebrate with you? What are you delighted at being celebrated for? What do they say? What do you feel? What are you pleased to have achieved over your life? What are you thrilled to have done, to have contributed towards. What skills are you most satisfied to have developed, and perhaps shared with others. What were some of the challenges you overcame? What skills and personal qualities do you have that enabled you to overcome those challenges?

Take a moment to jot down the new information that you discovered doing this activity. The outputs from these activities will develop into your vision.

The second activity is about developing an *away from*, thinking about what changes you want to make to your life.

ACTIVITY   Most feared obituary

Pretend that you have failed to change unhealthy and unhappy patterns that you have now. Project into the future how these problems will get worse as you get older and die. The most feared obituary is based on living a long life without any positive changes in your current standards, priorities and goals. In fact, problems can be expected to get much worse over the many years that you 'let yourself go' and deteriorate, and do nothing to make your life happier and healthier in any way. Next pretend to write your obituary just before you die. This is a very personal and detailed obituary for all of your friends and family to see.

Source: Hefferon, workshop presentation, 2010

This second activity may have given you different insights into some of the key things about your life that you would like to change. Make a note of them whilst they're still clear. If having done that, you're left with a slightly unpleasant feeling then stand up or stretch.

Why knowing your values is important

Values are the 'deep' criteria by which we make decisions, they are the things that we hold to be important, and for many they can be outside our awareness, held at a deep level. Values can be our compass for navigating through any complexity. Grant (2006) notes: 'You never get to West, but you can be headed in that direction.'

Values are also at work in more simple and routine decisions, even the most routine decisions will be influenced by our underlying values. For example, in a simpler situation ask yourself repeatedly the question, 'What's important to me about that?' After a couple of repetitions of the question you'll typically uncover the underlying value.

If you can't think of a more interesting decision, reflect on your choice of lunch and ask yourself, 'What's important to me about that?' Even when people appear to 'do' the same thing, their values or reasons for doing so might be different. For example, two people might bring their own lunch to work. One might have a value around economizing; the other may have values around eating wholesome, nutritious food.

Two people may accept similar roles within an organization – however, their underlying rationale for accepting the role might be very different. One person might have taken a job, and sees it as a long-term role, and enjoys the familiarity and mastery that experience brings. Another person may see the role as a stepping stone to something larger, an opportunity to learn and move on.

Knowing your values is motivating

Research by Schwartz (2005) has found that just knowing our values can be motivating. The more easily a value comes to mind, the more it will be activated. Then the ability to act according to our values on a daily basis can be motivating.

Some people just 'know' their values and live by them on a daily basis. If that's you, congratulations. However, in my experience the larger majority of people are less aware of their values.

For some the process of being explicit in finding 'what's important' can be very enlightening, and for others the conscious act of prioritizing their values can be of most use. How do you find your values? Read on.

Values sort

The way I prefer to work with my clients is to use a pack of values cards, available at: **www.thebusinessofchange.co.uk/free-personal-development.**

Before describing the short sequence of steps to carry out with the cards, it's useful to gain a bit of background on what otherwise might seems like trivial points that could get missed in your enthusiasm to start the activity:

- keep the context in mind;
- sit on the floor;
- use the different labels of importance to develop granularity;

This activity is important because it's all too easy for our values to become a bit hidden behind some of the pressures and demands of others. Remember the benefits of tapping into your intrinsic motivation – finding your values is a step in that process.

Here's more on each of the above points.

Context

In what context are you thinking about values? For example, are you thinking about the value in the context of work, home, sport? I encourage my clients to write down and have visible the context in which they're thinking about their values. Much research has shown that in different settings, different values can become more important.

For example, the value of 'competition' might be supremely important to you in the sporting arena, but perhaps at work a higher value is 'helping others'. So keeping the context visible is a reminder that the value may still be important to you – but perhaps not as important in this context.

Sit on the floor

I highly recommend you sit on the floor to do the initial values sort. Sitting on the floor connects you to a more childlike energy which can tap into a more natural, playful side. Sitting at a desk can inadvertently encourage 'proper' behaviour, perhaps encouraging values that one thinks 'should' be important. The central idea here is to assist you to find *your own values*.

Different groups

To aid sorting your values, use five different labels (from 'not at all important' to 'extremely important to me'). This gives a graded differentiation rather than just two extremes (see Figure 4.6).

FIGURE 4.6   A values sort

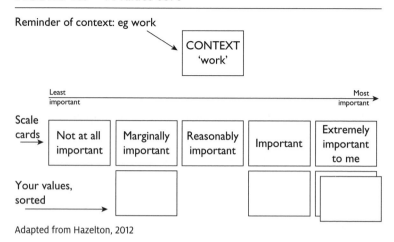

Adapted from Hazelton, 2012

ACTIVITY   Sorting your values

1 Choose the context (eg work) for which you want to find your values.

2 Put the scale cards in order. Then take a values card, read it, and use your gut instinct to put it in one of the groups. Take just a couple of seconds per card (and even if you're a slower reader, I suggest no more than 10 seconds per card).

3 Repeat for all of the cards. By the end the cards should be distributed across the groups, reflecting which your strongest values are.   ·

Finding your top eight values

Once sorted, identify your top eight values. Even if you have significantly more than eight in your 'extremely important to me' group this can be a quick and easy process to find the *most* important. If you can, go with your intuition as to which are the most important.

What if you have more than eight in this group?

If you have more than eight values in the 'extremely important to me' pile you may want to move values in the other piles to one side, and do another sort of just these values. Getting clarity about your most important values does seem in itself to provide personal insight. Sometimes prioritizing (described on page 93) is the only way people can decide which eight are their most important.

The higher ranked a value is, the more likely that a person will form an 'action plan' around it.

What if you have fewer than eight in this group?

It's not for me to judge how many values you need for it to be effective. If you would like to increase the number, then you could look at 'promoting' others from the next group so that you've got a top eight. Note however that one of the later steps is prioritizing values so you may want to keep your newly promoted values slightly separate, as it's likely they'll have a lower priority than some of the others.

Prioritizing

When you have your top eight values, put them in a hierarchy. Some people find they can do this intuitively (and have automatically done this), whilst others need a more systematic process, but this should take no more than 10 minutes.

ACTIVITY   Prioritizing

Take one card, and place it face up. Take the next card, and ask yourself if X is more important than Y, and place it in order with the highest at the top. Repeat for the next card, and so on.

Write them down in priority order and date the list. Trust me on this point: you may find yourself coming back to the list and it's useful to have a record.

Values conflict

There are several areas in which values can conflict:

- Sometimes a person can't decide which order the values are in, which can cause 'intra-psychic' conflict. ('Part of me wants to do this, part of me wants to do that' – you now have your values hierarchy, and know their relative importance.)

- Or it can seem that values are diametrically opposed (job security vs career adventure).

- In addition to these conflicts within us, there can also be value conflicts between people. When an agreement is reached by two or more people, if the decision has been made on different sets of values, longer term there may be differences of opinion or actions. This is beyond the scope of this book.

Intra-personal conflict

Schwartz (2005) has demonstrated that there are 10 basic values. I tend to use a broader list with my clients as some of the terminology in Figure 4.7 can be a bit off-putting. Schwartz suggests that the closer any two values in either direction around the circle, the more similar the underlying motivation. The more distant any two values, the more the underlying motivations are different.

Let's take an example where a person has to decide to work a couple of extra hours on an important project, or leave to spend time with their family. What decision do they make?

It's quite easy to see that different people may have different underpinning values – but for this example, the value underpinning staying late on the project could be achievement for one, stimulation for another, or job security for yet another.

In a situation like this, a person who has prioritized their values is more likely to know what's most important to them when making the decision.

Bringing it together

During this chapter, you've thought about your lifetime goals, you've projected yourself to the future, you've thought about what your obituary will sound like if nothing changes, indeed a slow decline happens. You've also considered your best possible future – celebrating your 80th birthday, and imagined others speaking about the things you're most proud to have achieved. You've taken practical steps to understand your values – the underlying criteria by which you make decisions. Now it's time to take a moment to bring these activities into a visualization. If you can imagine going to the shops to buy a pint of milk then you can visualize: so let's get on with it.

FIGURE 4.7   Trade-offs among values

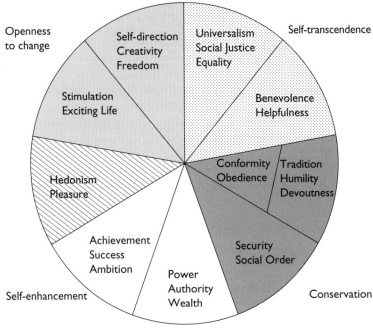

Source: Schwartz (2005)

ACTIVITY   Visualization

Often when people visualize they like to close their eyes, but it's not essential. Many people 'see' the picture and find it easiest to start with that, but if you can start with the sounds of success, or the feelings of success and if you can include all three (sights, sounds and feelings) that's ideal. Hold the picture. Then work back: visualize yourself preparing for your goal in a way that will lead to maximum success. It's important to see yourself making step-by-step progress towards meeting your goal.

If you prefer, you can listen to an audio file of me reading these steps, downloadable on the website (www.thebusinessofchange.co.uk), so that you can immerse yourself in the visualization.

If you're ready to close your eyes, do it now. Take a couple of deep breaths. Very good. Take a moment to think about what success means to you. Visualize success! What do you see? ... What else? ... Brighten the colours for a moment. Who's there with you? Tune in to what they're saying. You may have to turn the sound up. Listen well. What else do you hear? Listen some more. Good ... now notice your feelings in this successful place. Notice any significant textures ... Good. What's the taste of success? Now take an extra moment to notice any significant smells? Now you have that visualization, hold it for a moment. Good.

Think back to the things you've done to achieve your success. What are some of the obstacles that you have overcome to get to where you are now? What are some of the obstacles that might have overwhelmed someone else – whereas you persevered? What are some of your key inner resources that allowed you to overcome these obstacles? What else? Now think of some of the practical things that you did to get where you are, and achieve your success. What did you do? What else? Who else supported you in your endeavours? How did you get them involved? How did you prioritize your time? Take as long as you need to absorb the key learnings. Good. And when you're ready, and only when you are ready gently bring your awareness back to the room and open your eyes.

Taking it forward

Remember the donkey at the beginning of the chapter – undecided about which bale of hay to choose. By now you will have some sort of vision for the future, and while it may only be a rough sketch, wherever you are with it is great. Your vision will start to provide you with clarity and direction around what's important to you.

Summary

- *Away from* goals provide the energy to change an unwanted situation, but to be really effective it's useful to also have a *towards* goal which gives you focus and direction.
- Although some people just seem to know what their vision and life purpose is about, for most of us creating a vision is a process which can take some time and thought.
- A number of different activities can be used as input to creating your vision.
- Having a long-term vision can keep you on track and moving forward when day-to-day tasks risk anchoring you to a particular spot.

- There are different flavours of motivation. Intrinsic motivation has been described as providing a 'powerhouse' of energy.
- Your values are the internal criteria by which you make decisions.
- Making your values explicit to you will help you make decisions.

More information

For a 10-minute animated clip on the findings of Dan Pink's book, *Drive: The surprising truth about what motivates us* see: http://www.youtube.com/watch?v=u6XAPnuFjJc&feature=youtu.be http://youblisher.com/p/7435-Self-Determination-Theory.

Notes

1 Known as distal goals.

2 I just know there's someone who will read this saying that the bi-directional wheels on roller-skates are only likely to produce travel in two directions – that's not you is it?!

3 I know the term 'energy' in this context can sound a bit new age, but scientists (Kappes and Oettingen, 2011) have experience of measuring 'energization' with measurements of autonomic function [the processes of the body which happen without conscious control], such as systolic blood pressure or cardiovascular response, because 'energization' leads to an increased demand for oxygen and nutrients that are supplied by the cardiovascular system.

Part Three
POWER TOOLS FOR A BETTER WORK LIFE

5
Time travel – time perspectives to increase your well-being

Have you ever noticed that some people seem to live in the past, and others are focused on the 'next big thing'? For people that live more in the past, you might have heard them discussing a previous project when 'things were different round here back then' or 'back in the days ...'. From people anticipating the future you're more likely to hear 'as soon as we reach that project milestone'. People have different orientations or perspectives in relation to time.

Until several years ago, although I knew that people had different perspectives when it came to time, I had assumed our time orientation or time perspective was 'just the way we're wired'. However, research shows that, when it comes to time, we *can* adjust our focus, ie we can choose which direction to face. Later I will talk about why you might want to choose your time perspective. Before you read further, so that you're uninfluenced by the theory of time perspectives, you may wish to take the Zimbardo Time Perspective

Inventory (ZTPI). It's a 61-item questionnaire and can be found at: **http://www.thetimeparadox.com/zimbardo-time-perspective-inventory/**

When you complete the online questionnaire you'll receive a set of five numbers. Without context these numbers don't mean much, but they are your current blend of time perspective 'scores'.

Figure 5.1 shows a graph, where the dots indicate what Philip Zimbardo and John Boyd (2008) suggest is the 'ideal' balance of time perspectives. For now simply plot your results on Figure 5.1, recognizing that whatever the chart looks like now, you can, if you wish, adjust your time perspectives – they're not set in stone!

If when you plot your score your number is above the dot then you have more of that particular time perspective than Zimbardo and Boyd consider ideal. If your plot is below their dot you simply have less than they consider ideal.

A huge amount of data has been collected on the time perspectives and the average score on each of the time perspectives is different. Whether your plot is above or below the 'ideal dot' you might be interested to know how your score stacks up against other people. The average score for each time perspective lines up with 50 per cent on the graph. For example, on the past negative time perspective, people's average score is 3.0. On the past positive it is 3.7.

For those of you interested in the scoring there is more information on the website.

(*Note*: Figure 5.1 and the ZTPI website show a score for transcendental future. There is a separate questionnaire available on the Time Paradox website which measures transcendental future or belief in

FIGURE 5.1   ZTPI ideal time perspectives

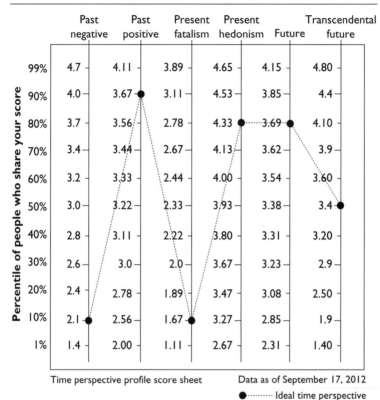

	Past negative	Past positive	Present fatalism	Present hedonism	Future	Transcendental future
99%	4.7	4.11	3.89	4.65	4.15	4.80
90%	4.0	3.67	3.11	4.53	3.85	4.4
80%	3.7	3.56	2.78	4.33	3.69	4.10
70%	3.4	3.44	2.67	4.13	3.62	3.9
60%	3.2	3.33	2.44	4.00	3.54	3.60
50%	3.0	3.22	2.33	3.93	3.38	3.4
40%	2.8	3.11	2.22	3.80	3.31	3.20
30%	2.6	3.0	2.0	3.67	3.23	2.9
20%	2.4	2.78	1.89	3.47	3.08	2.50
10%	2.1	2.56	1.67	3.27	2.85	1.9
1%	1.4	2.00	1.11	2.67	2.31	1.40

Percentile of people who share your score

Time perspective profile score sheet   Data as of September 17, 2012

●·········· Ideal time perspective

Source: www.thetimeparadox.com/surveys

life after death. However, it's beyond the scope of this book, and is not discussed further.)

What follows is a brief overview of six different time orientations, which excludes transcendental future, but includes holistic present which is not currently measured on the ZTPI. Then I'll explore research which shows that a 'balanced time perspective' is the most effective for your well-being and ultimately for having great days at work. With this research in mind, you might be inclined to do some 'time travel' and change the balance of your current time orientations – so I'll then go into more detail and show you some simple ways to start to adjust your time orientations. Any time travelling you do doesn't have to be permanent, but it will ultimately give you the choice of selecting the most appropriate perspective to suit the situation! Just knowing you have a choice of time perspectives can make an impact.

Overview of time perspectives

Past, present and future orientations are the three major time orientations. However, within each orientation there are some not so subtle nuances which affect how we feel, how proactive we are, and our experiences of life. For example; we can think about the past in positive ways (described as past positive) or in more negative ways (described as past negative). There are three different ways in which we can experience the present moment, from a person who throws themselves joyously into the moment (hedonic), to someone who has a more mindful approach (holistic), to someone who has a more fatalistic outlook. Currently the research indicates just two future orientations: future and a transcendental future – although I suspect that on-going research will find different flavours of future from someone who projects catastrophe in the future through to a more optimistic future outlook.

The Zimbardo Time Perspective Inventory (ZTPI) measures five of the six time perspectives: past negative, past positive, two shades of present (present hedonism, present fatalism), as well as future. What follows is a short summary of each of them, and I expect that to a greater or lesser degree you will recognize each time perspective. After these short summaries we look at the best balance for having great days at work, followed by suggestions for adjusting your perspectives.

Past negative

At an extreme, you will recognize that some people can turn any past experience into a negative. For example, one couple I know, when asked about the best meal they've ever had, turned it into 'well I don't know about that, but we've have had some awful meals

... do you remember that meal where...', and they continue to describe the worst meals they've had. I've chosen a non-work example because it would be too easy to look for possible rational justification defending an individual's work situation.

Take the following examples. A promotion, which should be an event to be celebrated, but it's too easy to focus on the longer hours and the increasing responsibility. A training course, which could be viewed as an opportunity to learn and develop, but how do you speak about it if the over-riding memory was of the poor location and inadequate catering services? The new IT system should provide more timely information to all involved, but for you personally it's of no value if you have to log on and submit a 'query' which takes time, whereas previously you just had to make a quick call to the depot.

In each of these individual cases there is of course an element of truth – the new IT system may take longer for an individual to use, and the benefits may not be seen directly by the individual but by the organization. The food on the training course may have been of poor quality, and the promotion may well have led to more responsibility and working longer hours. However, the thing to notice is whether 'past negative' is a theme for you.

Whilst at work, reminders of what didn't work can be useful in ensuring that costly mistakes aren't repeated. However, it can have a demoralizing effect on colleagues, often undermining successes (yours and theirs) along the way.

Past positive

By contrast you may recognize people who seem to look back at the past through rose-tinted spectacles, only seeing the good in events. When others use this perspective, I've sometimes found them to be living in a romanticized past. However, research shows that a past positive time perspective (Boniwell *et al*, 2010) seems to be a key element in living a happy life. It's important to be able to savour past experiences, to reminisce and remember the good times.

Present hedonism

Typically when we talk of someone living in the present we refer to them enjoying the pleasures in life, they don't like to wait for anything, preferring instant gratification. They typically have high energy. One downside is that they can have weak impulse control, ie they live for today often not thinking about the consequences for tomorrow. This can lead to them taking risks with their future, often around health.

Present fatalism

Fatalism is more typical of someone who feels they have no choices in life. Zimbardo gives the example of an uneducated parent, with children doing poorly in school, a son mixed up with drugs and gangs and a pregnant teenage daughter. With rent overdue and currently seeking work this person might believe they have no chance of improving their life, and therefore may have beliefs that 'my path is controlled by forces I cannot influence'. This is the fatalistic time orientation.

Holistic present

The holistic present is a healthy perspective to have. 'The past and future are abstractions, mental constructions that are subject to distortion, wishful thinking, and the psychological disorders of depression, anxiety and worry' (Zimbardo and Boyd, 2008).

The holistic present is neither a slave to the past nor a means to the future, it reflects neither the pleasure seeking of present hedonism nor the cynicism and resignation of present fatalism. Sometimes the concept of holistic present is described as mindfulness. Sadly this is not measured by the ZTPI.

The future

The future is never experienced directly; it is another psychologically constructed mental state. Becoming future oriented involves a focus on discipline, working hard today for the successes of tomorrow. Zimbardo and Boyd make the point that no one is born with a future time perspective; it's been learned, and those people who have successfully been through the education system have developed a stronger future time perspective. Often it's goal orientated.

Which perspective do you use and which is best?

These very short portraits will have given you a taster of different time perspectives. Even if you haven't taken the questionnaire, instinctively you might know which one, or ones, are most prevalent within you. We seem to be a mix of perspectives and there seems to be a combination of perspectives which is better for our well-being and having great days at work.

You might wonder which combination of time perspectives is 'best', and a team of researchers (Boniwell *et al*, 2010) explored exactly that question. The researchers suggested that having a single time perspective could become dysfunctional, and found four distinct patterns or blends of time perspectives: future orientated, present orientated, balanced and negative.

They found that people who have a 'balanced time perspective' have higher levels of well-being, find more meaning in life and they enjoy life more. They define a balanced time perspective as high scores on past positive, present hedonistic and future, and low scores on past negative and present fatalistic. This is the 'ideal', which is shown as the dots on the ZTPI (see Figure 5.1). They noted that having a high future time orientation is only conducive to well-being within the context of a balanced time perspective, when it is balanced by present hedonistic and past positive.

Knowing that a particular set of time perspectives are best for your well-being you might want to know how you can make small adjustments to become mentally fitter without going near a gym. Therefore, it's developing the balanced time perspective that I'll focus on.

Making changes to your time perspective

This section describes how you could choose to make changes to your time orientations. Logically we tend to think of things in terms of past, present and future. However I suggest a sequence for implementing them which starts by developing awareness of the present – and therefore I describe them starting with present, past then future. Really the present is the only moment we have and other orientations can enhance or contaminate the present moment.

The sequence I suggest when adjusting your time perspective is: first increase your moment-to-moment awareness so that you know which time perspective you're using, then decrease past negative orientation because it's so insidious. By addressing these challenges head on you can bring immediate benefit in terms of a happier life and better health. This will give you some mental space to increase your past positive experiences and finally maximize your future goal-setting orientation.

Until coming across this research I had discounted any value from 'past' events, whether it was the past positive rosy glow, or the past negative taint. I had focused instead on both the here and now, and the future. However having found this research I've embraced the balanced time perspective, which for me incorporated more past positive experiences. Personally I've benefited from it, and I hope it provides you with a different approach.

Present

Insanity: doing the same thing over and over again and expecting different results.

Albert Einstein

There are two main elements in this section: mindfulness and flow. They are almost opposites. Flow is about getting lost in the experience and in the moment, whereas mindfulness is about developing awareness in the moment, so that you have increased awareness of what's going on both inside yourself and around you. With increasing awareness you can make conscious and perhaps different choices. You may have come across the quote above from Einstein, suggesting it's insane to constantly repeat something expecting different results. Developing your present holistic time perspective will give you increasing awareness and new information. Mindfully choosing your thoughts and actions may lead you to different decisions and different actions. However, mindfulness doesn't come naturally for most people.

Contaminants of mindfulness

For most people, moment-by-moment awareness doesn't come naturally. No matter how much they would like a clear or quiet mind, they find that thoughts distract them. This is very common, so let's explore some of the contaminants of enjoying the present moment (hedonic) or mindfulness (holistic), and explore the things that can cloud the mind.

The terms *reachback* and *afterburn* are probably not ones with which you're familiar (Berne, 1971). However, I think they richly encapsulate many people's experiences of what stops them being mindful.

You've experienced afterburn if you've noticed that occasionally after 'something happens' you find yourself spending more mental energy thinking about it than you would like. For example, if you get some critical feedback about a piece of work and you continually re-play it then the event is causing afterburn. Chapter 9 describes some strategies for coping with set backs.

Reachback is when you worry about something that has not, and possibly will never happen. However, this expected or anticipated event takes your attention and you spend time 'worrying' about it. The event is said to be reaching back, and affecting you in the present moment. For example, you might be concerned about preparing for and delivering an important presentation.

Therefore the terms 'reachback' and 'afterburn' simply describe how our mental processing in the present moment can sometimes be full of anticipated anxiety from a future event, or post-event anxiety. Filling your brain's processing power with these contaminants takes away your mental processing power. Even if you're not so interested in your brain's processing power, it's likely these contaminants mean that we're not living rich and fulfilling lives in the present. As you become more aware of the present, you can become increasingly aware of what's gnawing at your attention. With that awareness you can do something about it.

If it's something from the past that needs attention or closure you can do this either alone or by seeking professional guidance. You can't change the past but you can change how you think and feel about it. The section on past negative and past positive gives a few more suggestions of how to change your thinking in this area.

If there's something in the future that's causing 'reachback', perhaps a more action-orientated approach might be beneficial. For example, what actions could you take? Sit down with paper and pen and decide what actions you will take. You may need to do some research, and finding out more information will take a little time to research. Perhaps there are plans you need to put in place: a person who 'just worries' without taking action is like a person in a boat that's letting in water who just worries about the water leaking in and doesn't start to bail. Worrying about a presentation but not taking action is the same. There are steps you can take, they may take some time to think about and enact but taking action will make more progress than worry.

You might be surprised how much mental energy you're burning with unresolved business and worry. You might say that it's worth worrying about a presentation next week. I suggest it's worth doing some more preparation.

One way to develop moment-by-moment awareness is through mindfulness. The easiest way to begin mindfulness is through mindfulness meditation. Like learning any new skill it takes practice.

Mindfulness meditation

Mindfulness is essentially about increasing your awareness, in a very accepting way. The term 'mindful meditation' can be off-putting: for some people just the word meditation conjures up images of sitting cross-legged for hours and chanting – and in my experience it isn't. This section is intended to give you a little more information about mindfulness meditation, Firstly, it demonstrates the benefits, then removes the mystique. Secondly, it gives you some facts and some pointers of where to find more information, including a link to a 10-minute guided mindfulness meditation should you decide to give it a go for yourself.

A review of the research around meditation can be found in Shapiro *et al* (2009). Meditation has been found to contribute to a broad range of benefits from memory and intelligence, creativity and interpersonal functioning, to improving self-esteem and well-being. The researchers found increases in empathy and measures of self-actualization as well as improving levels of trust and increasing measures of spirituality. They found improvements in measures of sense of coherence and stress hardiness. They noted too that there were measurable physiological benefits associated with meditation. Whilst these findings were wide ranging, they caveated them by noting limitations in the research methodology.

Further to the above, Sedlmeier and his colleagues (Sedlmeier *et al*, 2012) undertook an extensive and rigorous meta-analysis of the meditation in non-clinical groups, examining research since 1970. Their overall conclusions, based on 163 studies, was that meditation is effective, showing improvements in a number of areas from memory and intelligence, through to creativity and interpersonal functioning, increases in self-esteem and overall well-being (p 7).

I've practised yoga for many years. My awareness started to increase around my posture, and straightening my spine. I subsequently came across HeartMath (**http://www.heartmath.com/**) which involves deep breathing for 90 seconds – the 'catch' is that it's repeated throughout the day, perhaps up to 20–30 times. Subsequently I came across mindfulness, which often starts with mindfulness meditation.

How do you increase your mindfulness?

On the **www.getsomeheadspace.com** website (see page 136 for the QR code) there are free, 10-minute, guided meditations which take you through the meditation sequence. Although the founder of HeadSpace, Andy Puddicombe, was a Buddhist monk, at no point does he encourage others to follow this path – his goal is to get people mindful through meditation.

Some people can be slightly fearful of the unknown, so I've described what happens in an initial meditation:

- Set a timer with a gentle alarm.
- Sit upright in a chair, feet flat on the ground, hands on or in lap.
- If you wish, close your eyes.
- Take a couple of deeper breaths.
- Take a couple of moments to mentally scan your body, noticing how it feels; you don't have to change anything.
- Any time you notice your thoughts have wandered, bring them gently back. Be kind to yourself.
- Stay aware of your breathing by gently having a tally: 1 for the in breath, 2 for the out breath, 3 for the in breath, 4 for the out breath, until you get to 10.
- Any time you notice your thoughts have wandered, bring them gently back. Be kind to yourself.
- Let thoughts come and let them go.

- Imagine a blue sky, with the thoughts as clouds – behind the clouds is a blue sky. Let the clouds come and go.
- Continue until the timer sounds.
- Bring your awareness back to your body.
- Open your eyes.

There is no substitute for experiencing it.

What is flow?

In contrast to mindfulness, flow (Csikszentmihalyi, 2002) is the time when you get lost in the moment. It happens when there's a fine balance between the challenge and your skills. It requires concentration to use your skills at their upper limits. There's research to suggest that people experience more flow at work than they would naturally predict. This is important because it's one of the aspects that make work enjoyable.

Csikszentmihalyi describes three conditions needed for flow: challenge, skill and feedback. The type of feedback required for flow is not the once-a-year appraisal, but moment-by-moment feedback. Perhaps it is easier to think of the type of feedback required for flow in a sporting context. It's not the feedback from the coach, it is what you observe or experience. In other words, if you're playing tennis it's the feedback that comes from how it feels when you are getting ready to hit the ball, through the feel of the ball striking your racket to seeing where it lands.

How do you get flow?

In the early stages of a new activity a coach or manager can assist with ensuring flow. They can manipulate the challenge to match (or slightly exceed) the skills of the individual.

When learning new skills we often start with something simple, before progressing to the more complex. Whether it's learning a new software package or the ubiquitous presentation, we often learn and have successes with the simplified version before increasing the challenge. For example, when learning to present we start in front of small groups first – generally for a few minutes at a time – before accepting larger, more formal events standing in front of hundreds of people. Learning a new software application is no different. We start with the simple, become adept at it, and then the requirement becomes more complex ... and we rise to the challenge.

A colleague recently asserted that the role of the manager is 'crucial in determining how much challenge someone can handle to help them experience more flow in their working life'. A good leader certainly plays a part in providing challenging opportunities whilst ensuring an individual has the skills required to meet the challenge. Too much challenge without skills leads to being overwhelmed and too many skills without the challenge leads to boredom and apathy. However, relying on your manager removes you from the equation – and I think you can ask for what you need in terms of new challenge or training.

Who's responsible for your flow experiences?

I believe you can take control of gaining more flow at work. You may need to develop skills to take ownership, develop self-awareness and improve your communication skills, so that you can ask for a greater or lesser degree of challenge. It's too easy to think 'my job is boring', and not to take any action, to push the responsibility onto someone else (outside of your circle of control). I've always thought that if I'm going to be at work then I might as well enjoy it. Being able to let your boss know you're not challenged also requires a good relationship between manager and employee where an employee can state how they feel (whether anxious or apathetic) to their manager. In my experience this is very much in line with expectations for self-regulation placed on employees in many businesses today.

Sadly some leaders don't have the skill, time or inclination for one-to-one development. I hope you have a great boss who provides you with challenges that are challenging but achievable, and ensures that you continue to have an appropriate level of challenge so that were asked not to participate in any flow activities. They quickly plunged into a state 'similar to a serious psychiatric disorder', requiring the experiment to stop after just two days. It seems that a state of flow is essential to our well-being. Remembering that flow is the balance of challenge and skill, with some feedback, take some time to consider where you find flow activities. Are there activities in which you would benefit from increasing the challenge, or increasing your level of skill?

Past

Having developed awareness in the present, I'll now delve into the past time perspective. There are two main types of past perspective: past positive and past negative. In my experience many people live in the past, often describing how they got to the current situation, and less attention is given to how to move it forward. First I'll describe how to stop or reduce past negative before focusing on increasing past positive, which forms part of a balanced time perspective and is good for well-being.

> It has been said that the abundant life begins when we give up all hope of ever having a better past. Many of us do not realize that clinging to the hope of a better past keeps us from finding meaning and purpose today. We covertly act as though if we are frustrated and unhappy enough about our regrets somehow life will take pity on us and undo them.
>
> Ulrich and Ulrich (2010)

Some people say that a past positive time perspective can paper over the gritty reality of the past, and therefore it's more delusional. I would contrast this by suggesting that past negative can also overlook some of life's enjoyable moments by focusing 'solely' on the negative.

Our memories are not 'videos' of events which make accurate recordings of our experiences. This is not how our memory works. There is significant research to show how easily memory becomes manipulated (Chabris and Simons, 2010; Loftus and Palmer, 1974, 1996). Professor Hood provides a useful metaphor for thinking about

you don't flip into either a state of anxiety or apath
you can ask and you do have other choices – see Cha_

If you are a manager and one of your employees is co_
saying they're bored, then first of all, congratulations o_
open and trusting relationships. As their manager you n
useful to work with them to identify their next challe
support them through the early stages. This is something \
can do which will benefit them and your department. Y
change the scope or increase their level of responsibility. It c
necessarily mean you have to give a promotion.

Of course challenge alone isn't motivating. Further research in
area by Fave and Massimini (2005) has shown two additio
'motivational variables, namely wishing to do the activity and t
relevance of the activity to future goals'. This is also where you hav
to be honest with yourself and think about your vision – what you
really want to do – and set yourself some goals to achieve them.
Goal setting is covered later in Chapter 7.

Many organizations have traditionally had a paternalistic streak,
'taking good care' of employees, many of whom had a 'job for life'.
In recent times this has changed to one where employees are encouraged to take more responsibility for their actions. With my clients
I use the 'parent, adult, child' model, from transactional analysis, to
describe the different dynamics between people. Traditionally managers were 'parental'. Employees took the role of 'child'. However,
organizations seem to be shifting to having a more adult-to-adult
approach which encourages a mature dialogue where employees
are encouraged to take responsibility. (More information on this
ego state model can be found in Stewart and Joines, 1987)

Peterson (2006) describes a similar authoritative style which 'leads
to employees who are independent yet responsible'.

No flow experience?

What if you don't get into flow experiences? Csikszentmihalyi (cited in
Pink, 2009) described where participants in a psychology experiment

memory. He suggests our store of memories is more like a compost heap than a DVD (Hood, 2012). Most of the contents of our memories turn to the compost equivalent of mush relatively quickly; it is just the odd piece which retains its form, taking longer to decompose.

Given our memories are not accurate recordings of the past, you can play an active part in creating and preserving past positive memories. It seems it's more about choice. Where do you point the video camera of the brain? You could choose to focus on the negative aspects or you could point it at the 'good bits'. First here's what you can do to reduce focus on the negative.

Past negative

The past negative time perspective is pervasive and insidious. It doesn't enhance your life, in fact it drains energy through the incessant negative talking about something that happened. There are different ways in which the past negative manifests itself, and there are different ways in which you can deal with it, with the goal to reduce levels of past negative thinking.

Firstly, I don't want to minimize a negative experience in the past. The intensity of people's experiences varies hugely from person to person. If issues or past experiences are deep seated, past negative has the potential to be a more challenging area to work through alone. For significant past negative experiences, trained counselling or psychotherapy professionals are available privately, sometimes through the NHS and through mental health charities.

Outside these deeply negative experiences there is much you can do on your own and this section covers three very different approaches that you can work through and use for yourself.

Firstly we will look at the ways to stop overthinking; secondly if you get caught up in the drama of storytelling about life's misfortunes there are some suggestions as to how to change your behaviour around storytelling. Finally we will look at an approach to searching for the benefit in the past negative experience.

Additionally meditation can be used to alleviate the weight of past negative experiences (see page 112).

Overthinking

There has been significant research on 'overthinking' and 'rumination'. Lyubomirsky (2010) describes this simply as 'thinking too much'. Overthinking is the needless, passive, excessive pondering of the meanings and causes of situations. Lyubomirsky, who has done extensive research in this area, goes as far as to say: 'If you're an overthinker, one of the secrets to your happiness is the ability to allay obsessive overthinking and to reinterpret and redirect your negative thoughts into more neutral or optimistic ones'.

Susan Nolen-Hoeksema (2003) describes a three-step approach: stop, act and avoid future traps.

Stop

As soon as you notice you are overthinking it's important to stop it. There are different ways to stop:

- Deliberately distract yourself, perhaps by listening to music that you enjoy or watching a funny YouTube clip or an enjoyable film.
- Say 'stop' and force thoughts of something very different, for example the steps to book your next holiday.
- Set aside some time specifically for rumination – so when the thoughts arise you can truthfully tell yourself that you'll spend time on it later.
- Talk to a friend – my suggestion would be that you 'time-box' your woes, but sometimes just sharing the problem means it's not as overwhelming as it perhaps first seemed (see also the section on storytelling on page 119).
- Write your ruminations and worries down. This could be in a handwritten journal or through a keyboard – how you do it doesn't seem as important as the act of writing down your thoughts which can get them in an order.

Act

Getting Things Done author David Allen (2001) advises approaching all tasks and projects by defining the very next step When you have a clear next step it becomes increasingly likely that you'll take action. My recommendation is to make the next step a small step, indeed keep all the steps small and maintain momentum to act by achieving them. There's more to follow on this topic in Chapter 7 on Goals.

Avoid future traps

Making plans for prevention can take a little bit of time and some awareness of what causes you to overthink. However, when you've discovered the type of event or situation that prompts your overthinking you can then avoid or modify the situations that trigger overthinking and rumination.

Storytelling

Occasionally when people recount their experiences of past negative situations, they're often met with gasps, sighs, aghast looks and comments akin to 'oh, that's so awful'.

With these responses, the 'storyteller' is being 'stroked': by stroked I mean that they're gaining attention for their well-honed formula of recounting stories which are typically past negative experiences. Past negative storytelling can be popular, especially if the individual also has a knack of dramatizing it or making it 'funny'. We all like to receive attention and 'strokes', and unwittingly the expectations and comments of friends, confidants and associates reinforce this past negative behaviour.

Some people make a living from this storytelling – and they do it deliberately, in a given context. However, for the rest of us it can become an addictive pattern of behaviour. It can seem harmless enough, but we're unconsciously looking out for the negative event to tell our next story: looking out for the negative becomes our focus. Stories are the way in which we construct meaning in our life. As one key researcher of stories (McAdams, 1992) suggests:

There can be no story without intention. Further there can be no intention without story.

The negative slowly gnaws away – reinforcing negative events. The first step is to know that you're doing it, and ideally to 'stop it'. Stopping past negative 'cold turkey' can be tricky because we've unwittingly trained others to 'expect' the negative ending. Your associates might be slightly disappointed not to hear your tales of woes, thus sub-consciously setting an expectation for you to 'revert' to the more expected past negative story next time. With friends it can be even harder as we seem to attract people like ourselves – and the basis of your relationships could be around these 'disaster' scenarios.

Take a moment to reflect on the effect of noticing and reliving, through your stories, the negative in life, as compared to the good in life. What impact is it likely to have long term? What effect does it have to have a store of 'you never guess what happened?' moments and memories which are typically past negative?

There is no quick fix for changing this habit. Developing a more mindful awareness, and making an active choice as to whether to recount your story is a great start. Creating new habits is discussed more in Chapter 8.

The final section on past negative is to actively look for benefits in the negative event or situation.

Benefit finding

One technique is that of 'benefit finding', that is finding benefit in a difficult life event (Tennen and Affleck, 2002).

In one experiment conducted by King and Miner (2000), participants were assigned to one of four conditions. One condition was a control group where participants were asked to write for 20 minutes about a mundane topic. The second group were asked to write about a traumatic event. The third group were asked to think about a traumatic event and then write about the positive aspects of that experience. Group four were asked to think about a traumatic event, and then spend the first 10 minutes writing about the traumatic event and then the next 10 minutes writing about the positive aspects of the event. All groups wrote for 20 minutes. The study was carried out over three days, after which participants signed release forms for access to medical records.

Findings from the research demonstrated that the control group showed the highest level of visits to the health centre. Whilst writing about the trauma and the benefits reduced the number of visits to the health centre, it was the group that wrote solely about the benefits who after five months showed a significant reduction in number of visits to the health centre. So writing about a traumatic event is useful and writing about the benefits has the highest positive impact on your health and well-being.

Although it may seem a bit depressing to think of the negative event, and then write about the positive benefits, the research also took before and after snapshots of participants' mood and the writing didn't seem to have an immediate impact in terms of mood – either positively or negatively. So if you want to find benefit, and perhaps gain closure, insight and wisdom from a past negative event, here are the instructions used in the experiment. It takes 20 minutes, and should be repeated on three consecutive days. There might be a situation at work that you feel slighted over, perhaps a promotion for which you were passed over that it might be useful to reflect on.

Please recall a traumatic life event or some loss you have experienced in your life. Think about the experience for a few moments. Now, focus on the positive aspects of the experience. Please write about how you have changed or grown as a person as a result of the experience. Focus on the positive aspects and how the experience has benefited you as a person – how has the experience made you better able to meet the challenges of the future? As you write, do not worry about punctuation or grammar, just really let go and write as much as you can about the positive aspects of the experience.

From the destructive, negative, storytelling patterns described previously, the benefit-finding approach seems to encourage a happier ending for a traumatic event, which has shown heightened physical health.

Next we move to the past positive time perspective. The focus is looking back and remembering the positive.

Past positive

From describing how to reduce our past negative time perspective, this section will offer some suggestions as to how you can increase your past positive time perspective. This has been shown to be an important element in having a balanced time perspective, and leads to a healthier life.

Essentially it's an activity which requires you to look back and take notice of the positive. Positive psychology has researched a number of interventions and many of them can be viewed as enhancing your past positive time orientation. You may be surprised at how simple these activities are. However, do not let their apparent simplicity belie their power and effectiveness (Seligman *et al*, 2005).

Three good things

Daily, make a note of three good things that have happened during the day. This could range from a positive comment from your boss, a co-worker or a customer through to something more tangible.

Gratitude

What are you grateful for? Your gratitude could be directed towards a person, an inanimate object (for example, your smartphone) or towards nature (the weather). You can express gratitude directly, write a letter to someone (whether or not you send it) or you could keep a gratitude diary. You might be grateful for the support and encouragement of your co-workers or your manager. You may feel grateful for your choice of profession, or the environment in which you work.

Three good things and gratitude are discussed in the next chapter.

Savouring

Savouring is the conscious enjoyment of an experience. Lyubomirsky (2010) suggests there are past, present and future aspects of savouring. The past is savoured by remembering past events, you savour the present by being mindful and you can savour the future by anticipating and looking forward to future events. She suggests the difference between savouring and flow is that whilst flow is about being fully immersed in the experience, savouring is about stepping outside the experience and reviewing it.

Having experienced the event, you can then relive that experience either alone or when you reminisce with friends. Chapter 10 describes the importance of social interactions, but for now, suffice it to say that in the same way people can amplify past negative experiences, it's useful to find people to amplify your past positive experiences. A shared experience can be fun, which is probably why we do so much past negative storytelling, but sharing a past positive event can be exhilarating – and more amazingly it can be learned!

Are you open to enjoying some of life's pleasures today? Does your busy schedule allow you to take a moment to take notice, to be in awe of nature? Do you see opportunities and occasionally take advantage of them – even if they're not on your to-do list today? When you do experience events are you primed to really notice and savour the experience, or does it just pass you by?

My partner had been travelling on business, and as he arrived home from one trip and before he took the next trip we decided to spend some 'quality time' together. We chose to go to the National Gallery in London. We picked the rooms to visit, and variously spent time both individually and together looking at and savouring the pictures and the experience.

We then went straight out for dinner and savoured and reminisced (past positive). I have to confess it was a very strange sensation; past positive was still pretty new to me. I wanted to scream, 'You were with me, why are we talking about this?' The positive experience of looking at the pictures and of sharing our favourites, of buying a postcard in the shop – with my partner sneaking to buy me a small blank notebook so that I wouldn't notice, but so that I could see it on my desk to be reminded of the experience – all of this is what has been etched on my brain.

For many people the thought of savouring at work might feel like it's beyond the elasticity of their imagination. Whilst there are plenty of times that you'll be in the flow, also catch yourself 'enjoying' work. The phrase 'enjoying work' is a bit counter culture in a society where the prevailing wind seems to be to moan. However, there may be moments when you're in meetings with colleagues and you appreciate (and can savour) their ideas, the collaboration and camaraderie. Perhaps it's when you provide an excellent service to a client; instead of brushing it off, take a moment and savour the pleasure. Others of you will get a thrill from solving problems; after the moment of 'problem solved', before dashing to find and solve the next one, allow a smile to cross your face and take a moment to savour the experience. Savouring can be done within the context of work.

Past orientation in business

Business is typically future focused – what's happening tomorrow, next week, next year. Business is about overcoming the challenges, solving problems, moving forward and gaining market share along the route to success. The popular view of business is that it's thrusting and forward thinking. It sounds very dynamic. For many people the day-to-day reality is somewhat different. When dealing with problems a past time focus seems to remove action in the moment, and dwell on causation – which is not useful for making progress towards a goal.

In business, when something that is commonly described an 'an issue' presents itself, it can become the melting pot of, amongst other things, different time perspectives. The time perspective of wanting to resolve the situation (in the future) sometimes sits uncomfortably alongside those who want to dig into the cause of the problem (which happened in the past). Both have a place, but too often in business the two perspectives collide.

Recently I wanted some information from an organization that I had contacted several months previously. As my deadline for gathering the information approached I redoubled my efforts. Eventually I was told that I couldn't be given the information for three more weeks (beyond my deadline). During the call I noticed that I wanted to focus on the solution, and focus on what could be provided within my timeframe, whereas the operative on the phone was intent on telling me that I hadn't followed their company's process and wanted to know why I had sent my original request to *that* person, rather than directly to him. I was focused on the future, and I realized the operative wanted to discuss the past, and attribute blame.

Sometimes to solve a problem it *is* useful to get to the bottom of what caused it, and ensure measures are put in place to prevent it happening again. This type of meeting might explore the 'systemic errors' or look at the 'root causes' with a view to implementing changes to prevent the situation from occurring again. It can be useful if everyone is metaphorically pointing in the same direction, looking at the past or towards the future.

In my experience root-cause meetings are very different from both resolving the immediate situation and daily conversations. Often conversations and meetings have strong elements of past negative, often with a bit of blame thrown in for good measure.

Einstein wrote that 'the formulation of the problem is often more essential than its solution'. It certainly seems that how something is formulated will direct attention in a certain way. For example, if the formulation of the question asks about the problem – you will probably get lots of information about the problem. 'How did the problem occur?' 'What's the cause of this frustration?' Whereas if you ask about the solution you might discover new ways of solving the problem. 'How could we solve the problem?' 'How could we overcome this frustration?'

> Imagine phoning a helpdesk with a problem about your new mobile phone. There are a range of options to start the conversation, from 'you've sold me a dud phone, your company is rubbish' (past focus with blame) to 'how do I receive a replacement?' (future/solution focus).

Whilst this example may be exaggerated, I've often seen the past blame orientation used in business (typically not to good effect). For a more productive outcome, I encourage clients to focus on the future outcome. Have clear goals and multiple pathways, remove any blame or attribution, and employ the 'getting things done' action of the second example.

I'm not suggesting you don't use the past perspective, but encourage you to do it with awareness, as many people get stuck discussing the past. Take an objective look at the following and consider which of the two perspectives is more likely to move the situation forward:

- Is the conversation about why the mobile phone doesn't work or about how to get a replacement?
- Is the conversation about why you didn't get the promotion, or what you need to do to get the promotion next time?
- Is the conversation about what has caused business to be so poor, or what you can do to generate interest in your business?

The major part of the above has been to bring awareness to the past negative perspective in business, because it is a major time and energy waster for you. In some business settings, the past positive may be more difficult to accomplish – this can be about taking time to celebrate and remembering success. You may need to employ a little creativity, to find ways in your environment to celebrate success, and perhaps even sneak in the occasional past positive memory.

However, a word of caution: 'Do you remember the good old times before the last department reorganization?'... this might initially sound like past positive, but contains elements of past negative in that the negative is the implicit or even explicit criticism that the department was better before the reorganization.

One useful tool is De Bono's six thinking hats (De Bono, 2000). The colour of each hat symbolizes a different perspective to take. When everyone is aware of the perspective of each hat, people can be directed to metaphorically wear different hats at different stages of the meeting. The benefit of an approach such as this is that people know that different perspectives will get covered, and the meeting can progress with group members looking in the same direction at the same time which can be more productive and a better experience. A similar approach to the hats could be used when considering time perspectives. Feedback can be given about the hat, rather than about the person – which seems to be easier for all involved. 'I notice a few people still wearing their grey, past negative hats. Can everyone now put on their purple future hats.'

Future

The best way to predict your future is to create it!

Abraham Lincoln

Chapter 4 discussed setting your vision, which encourages you to think about your future, and start to create it. One activity was to think about your 80th birthday and your achievements. A key element of the future time perspective is the ability to set and achieve goals. Goals are covered more fully in Chapter 7. After exploring catastrophization – where people worry and imagine a negative chain of events happening in the future – I then return to thinking about your future by touching on retirement.

It may be odd that a book entitled *Great Days at Work* discusses retirement, but to quote Stephen Covey, 'begin with the end in mind', and since retirement follows work that's the 'end' I would like to invite you to consider.

I will invite you to take a cursory look at your retirement. Depending on where you are in your career this might be very long term – and much can change between now and then – or a much shorter timescale whereby you might think there's not much time left to make changes or provisions for your future. I've discovered that there's never an ideal time to consider how you want to retire.

As described earlier, events in the future can reach back and affect us in the present moment. This reachback can range from mild worry to full-blown catastrophization where, based on one event, a chain reaction occurs and it all ends in disaster, and the 'worst possible outcome'. I've already suggested that taking action is one way to address some of the milder worries, but what about catastrophization?

Catastrophization

If you find when considering change that your brain races un-prompted to 'what if' scenarios with disastrous consequences, then the habit to break is that of catastrophization. A catastrophic set of links that a person might make when preparing for a presentation is something like this: *If you fluff the presentation, your boss will think you're a fraud, she'll dismiss you at the first opportunity, you won't be able to get another job, you won't be able to pay your mortgage, you will lose your home, you end up divorced, no access to the kids and living in a shelter for the homeless.*

With a set of links like that, no wonder some people dread presentations! Of course it's not just presentations. Reivich and Shatté (2002) found that when people catastrophize there is generally a pseudo-logical set of links. In order to combat this pseudo-logic, one way is to make a note of the links, and then consider the probability of each event happening.

Taking the above example, perhaps there's a 50 per cent likelihood of fluffing the presentation (you could take immediate action to reduce this percentage), then consider if, based on this one event, your boss will consider you a fraud. She may be disappointed – but a 'fraud'?

What's the likelihood – perhaps 1 in 100? Then consider how likely you are to be dismissed based on one poor presentation ... and so on.

By the end of the activity you should logically realize that the probability of the 'worst possible outcome' is very low. Strangely, seeing it written down can be enough to stop this catastrophization. However, there is an additional step

Reivich and Shatté suggest looking at the best possible outcome as a result of the event. Challenge yourself to come up with a 'what if' in which it turns out that not only do you come up smelling of roses, but you 'save the day'. Show the chain of events, and assign probabilities again: *Your presentation simply wows your manager, the CEO hears of your stunning presentation, and comes to make you an offer you can't refuse (whatever that might be). You accept the offer, you become an overnight success ...*

Then think about the likelihood of each step happening; you might find they have similar probabilities as the catastrophization scenario. Neither the disaster scenario nor the 'save the day' scenario is likely to be accurate. You will see that there's a pretty equal chance of both positive and negative events happening. Most of us can look at the positive event and see 'that's unlikely' – and this activity simply provides balance as we seem to get caught up in the negative much more easily than in the positive.

Psychologist Paul Rozin notes (in Kahneman, 2012) that in a bowl of cherries, one cockroach is likely to spoil it (the one negative in the positive). He also suggests that one cherry in the bowl of cockroaches does not make the cockroaches any more appealing. The impact of the negative is far greater than the positive. You can mitigate against risk, and put plans in place – and really focus on getting positive experiences.

Thinking about the future includes both long-term and short-term planning, and often we limit our thinking to achievements at work. However, a long and healthy retirement is a strong possibility for many of us, and it's useful to take some time to think about how we want to spend life after work. There may be plans or actions you can put in place now which would both enhance your life today and throughout your retirement.

Retirement

The best time to plant an oak tree was one hundred years ago. The second best time is today.'

Anon

So why think about retirement at all? Firstly, for those of us *not* on a final salary pension scheme, it's likely that the money we've put into our pensions won't be as much as we vaguely expected – so it can be useful to understand the implications, and if necessary to take appropriate action. This is not financial advice. If you have specific questions related to your pension please contact your independent financial advisor.

I've met people who complete their lottery ticket on a weekly basis and idly wish for a better future, without taking any action to plan for it. As the odds of winning the jackpot are just less than 1 in 14 million, the majority of us will need to have additional plans in place.

Secondly, knowing how you want to spend your retirement can provide direction and motivation for your days at work. Perhaps there's something that you plan to do in your retirement that you could plan to begin sooner that would lead to greater fulfilment.

Said in another way, not only do you get a chance to make financial plans but you can work on any life skills you might need. If you want to move to France then you have time to explore exactly where and start learning the language. This also gives you the opportunity to enjoy and experience aspects of your goals before you fully retire, adding to your life now: after all, who knows what's round the next corner?

Financial planning for your retirement

Neither economics nor history are my specialist topics, but let me take a moment to briefly outline the historical context for pension schemes and why most of us may want to be more proactive about decisions surrounding our retirement.

Pension schemes were initiated at a time when the population was increasing. This essentially meant that there were more people paying into the schemes than there were people receiving pensions. When pension schemes were first introduced life expectancy was lower than the retirement age. Therefore, although people paid into their pension they often died prior to retirement.

Over the past 50 years there have been significant improvements in healthcare which have contributed to increased life expectancy. People are living longer into their retirement and receiving state benefits. Peculiarities in stock markets and the escalating price of residential property has meant that many people have the funds to retire early.

In the UK the formal age for retirement has begun to increase. People in the UK are living longer and so, as the press are fond to point out, we have an aging population. Not as many of the younger generation are coming into the workforce, and they are paying pro-portionally fewer taxes (taxes which contribute to the state pension provisions). Whilst many of us had expectations of early retirement, the reality is that the state retirement age is increasing. This means we're likely to be working longer, perhaps up to 10 years longer. There are two main things to consider; how we want to spend our time at work, and how we want to spend our retirement. The latter is the focus for the next section, and may inform how we spend our time at work.

> At the time of writing this I'm 41. I remember people taking early retirement in their 50s. Certainly as soon as I started a job, I was encouraged to invest in my pension – and had my retirement age 'set' at 55. The UK state retirement age for me is now 67 – a 10-year difference.

The full stop

Traditionally in the West, we've had 'a work hard before you play' approach to retirement. This 'full stop' approach to work has been familiar in the West and Zimbardo and Boyd (2008) sum it up:

*In a sense, retirement is like the first day of summer break from
school, eagerly awaited until the second day, when you realize there's
a long quiet time ahead.*

However, there are alternatives to this traditional approach which
it is perhaps healthy to explore.

Retirement alternatives

What seems to be clear is that positive ageing starts well before
retirement. In retirement as in 'work life' people have different en-
vironmental conditions in which they will thrive. Some people will
thrive by having a clear purpose, others by harnessing their creativity. Perhaps we'll see people retiring around 65, taking 10+ years
'out' of work before looking for a new hobby or challenge in their 70s.

How one spends one's retirement is not prescribed – here are some
alternatives I found.

The never stop

Another approach to ageing and retirement is when the elders are
still involved in the community. In *Flow* (Csikszentmihalyi, 2002)
there's a description of 76-year-old Serafina working the land, living
in the community with blurred lines between work and play – she
loves what she does and can't imagine doing anything different!

I'm developing a lifestyle that is more akin to this – when it's work
for love, or the sheer curiosity of it, is it really work?

The seven-year stop

I came across an approach from a graphic designer, Sagmeister,
who in a TED talk (see end of chapter for link) describes mixing
'retirement', or time off, into working life by taking a sabbatical
every seven years.

He describes each sabbatical as reinvigorating and providing him
with enough creative ideas to carry him through the next seven
years. This assumes that one's doing work that one enjoys, and is
excited by the prospect of continuing, and in a profession whereby
such time away is possible.

The boomerang

Some people will retire and then return to some form of work, either through choice or necessity. Let's explore choice.

There's already a website (**www.yourencore.com**) specifically designed to recruit the brain power of retired scientists and engineers.

The book *Wikinomics* (Tapscott and Williams, 2008) describes a new age of collaboration, and how organizations are 'outsourcing' problems. Traditional outsourcing is typically a predefined service (eg helpdesk) moving to a typically lower-cost economy (eg India). However, in *Wikinomics* what's described are situations where companies define the problem (where to mine for gold; new ways of producing a chemical compound more cheaply), and interested individuals can then set their minds to solving these problems. Companies pay for solutions they use.

Wikinomics describes a retired chemist (p 97) with his years of experience able to solve the challenge of producing a particular chemical compounds more cheaply: 'The company was delighted ... and Mueller [the retired chemist] was $25,000 better off.' The real drive was not money – but his passion for chemistry. Some people seem to know their passion from an early age, and for others it unfurls through their life – but it seems that passion for 'something' can keep us motivated and engaged up to and into our retirement. How clear are you on what's your passion?

Passion at work may not be for everyone. One senior manager I spoke with said she realized that it's OK not to be totally in love with your job and that it's still possible to have great days at work. The trick in her case is that she's developed a great work–life balance, working flexible hours. She's accepted that she's not going to have a vocational career and has consciously decided to accept the advantages of her actual career (with benefits such as salary, flexible hours, good holidays etc). She's able to have great days without constantly hankering after the 'in love with my job' feeling.

Wisdom used to be a virtue commonly attributed to elders. How much richer our society would be if there were more ways to help society's elders give back or release their wisdom. Within the UK there are examples of communities of seniors supporting school children with reading – which is good for the child and the elder. It develops the child's reading skills and thus the future generation, but also values society's elders, providing them with mental stimulation, a sense of purpose and worth.

Staying young in mind
The TV programme *The Young Ones* (McDonald and Langer, 2010) showed six celebrities in their 70s and 80s. For one week they lived, worked and ate as if it were 1975 (their heyday) to see if they could 'regain' their youth. A similar earlier experiment by Langer had shown that because participants' minds were actively engaged in living 20 years earlier, their bodies seemed to follow. Langer believes:

This is a demonstration of how our bodies don't let us down as we get older, it's our minds that accept the labels of ageing. Freeing ourselves from that state of mind can turn back the clock.

(Western) society, it seems, has an expectancy of frailty and decrepitude in older life, with road signage showing hunched figures with the word 'elderly'. With messages like these reinforced frequently it's often hard to believe there is a more positive stereotype. Often 'celebrations' of those that reach 100 are from nursing homes which offer a bitter-sweet take on old age. Compare this to Asian societies where age and implied wisdom is venerated.

An article in *The Sunday Times* (Rogers and Angelini, 2011) entitled 'Life begins at 90' stated that there is an 'estimated 900,000 people already over 65 who are destined to live to be 100'. The article cited a marathon runner and body builder in their 90s, along with yoga guru BKS Iyengar who is also in his 90s. I found these compelling senior role models.

There is a saying that 'exceptions prove the rule', and none more so than in scientific exploration. Stanovich (2010) cautions against the use of single cases by saying 'case studies and testimonials are virtually worthless as evidence for the evaluation of psychological theories and treatments'. Perhaps these individuals are exceptions to the normal ageing process, but as with studies of peak performance, perhaps there is something to be learned from them too.

Vaillant, in Chapter 34 (p 573) of *Positive Psychology in Practice* (Linley and Joseph, 2004) dispels myths on factors that are not contributory to positive ageing (eg ancestral longevity), as well as citing seven factors that contribute to positive ageing (ie not smoking after age 45, healthy weight, exercise, stable marriage, education, mature defences and no misuse of alcohol).

Retirement certainly will cause most people to face their own mortality and if they are fortunate enough to discover or rediscover their creativity and a passion for life-long learning, then wisdom cannot be far off. The research shows that there are things you can do today to plan for a great and healthy retirement.

I suspect just knowing which time perspective you're stronger in and which you'd like to develop will be a positive start on your journey to change. However, you may want keep a regular (daily or weekly) journal of your progress.

Summary

- Time perspectives are really just a fancy way of saying some people look back, some experience the present, and some people look forward. The reality is that we typically do a bit of each.

- Research has shown that there are benefits of increased well-being from a time perspective which contains elements of past positive, holistic present and future.

- You can take active steps to develop your positive time perspective in a work environment.

- Sometimes with thoughts about the past and future cramming into our minds it can be harder to develop awareness.

- With increased awareness, we have more choice (rather than acting on automatic pilot).

- Mindfulness meditation is one way to develop this present awareness.
- Our work contains large elements of flow – the fine balance of our skills and the challenge. Do you need to up the challenge in your work to give you more flow?
- Many of us need to reduce the amount of time we spend in past negative – which also puts us back in our circle of control.
- Find ways at work to increase your past positive experiences – what do you enjoy – take a moment to savour the experience.
- Thinking about how we want to spend our future can affect our decisions today.

More information

In addition to taking the ZPTI Survey, if you want to know more about time perspectives read *The Time Paradox* by Zimbardo & Boyd.

To get started with free meditation take a look at the *Get Some Headspace* website: **http://www.getsomeheadspace.com/Tools**

Take a look at the seven-year sabbatical from Stefan Sagmeister: **http://www.ted.com/talks/stefan_sagmeister_the_power_of_time_ off.html**

6
Emotions at work – focusing on useful emotions

Whilst emotions have their place, typically that 'place' is not the workplace. In many workplaces the unwritten rule seems to be to leave emotions at the door and focus on logic.

'Emotions? At work? Oh no! Is this going to be a chapter on tree hugging?' I can almost hear the shrillness of the question, the fear – which, if it were true, would be an emotion at work.

For many the topic of 'emotions' is taboo in the workplace. However, emotions provide important information about ourselves and our well-being as well as giving us clues about other people, whether in terms of observable behaviours in response to our ideas as well as their demeanour. Most forms of employment involve working with others at some point during the day, so in order to have a great day at work, don't ignore the information that emotions provide you with about other people.

I've always thought that if I'm going to spend a significant amount of time at work, I might as well enjoy it. I've had a focus on my work, and over the years I've aimed to do more of what I enjoy.

However, more importantly, there are specific actions you can take to give *you* more positive emotions. This is important because positive emotions have been found to be a factor that causes both individuals and teams to thrive. It would be reasonable to expect that great days at work will include some positive emotions, which they do – but I'll start by describing the importance of all emotions.

Emotions can be like the stream of content delivered via television. Some people make active choices as to what to watch; some may randomly press buttons on the remote control hoping to get 'something better'; and there may be another group of people who may not have realized that they have control and channels *can* be changed. This chapter provides a guide to your 'emotional viewing' in three sections, which can be summarized as follows:

1 We have access to a full range of emotions.

2 These emotions provide value when they're authentic but not all emotions are authentic.

3 We need to increase our positive authentic emotions.

What follows is a short experiment to see how easily you can affect your emotions. Try this for yourself.

Think of a bad day at work; take a moment to think of what made it bad. As you think of the memory – how do you feel now? (Pause) Don't languish too long on that memory. Shake off the memory by remembering what you had for breakfast.

Now think of a good day at work; what factors contributed to it? How did you feel? (Pause) How do you feel now?

Most people find that they can remember and experience, to a greater or lesser extent, both positive and negative emotions. The good news is that you can consciously switch between emotions very quickly. By further developing and using this skill you can have a huge impact on your emotional well-being.

A range of emotions

There's a full range of emotions available to us. Most of us recognize an extensive catalogue of emotions which might include shame, guilt, anxiety, envy, depression, frustration and more positively contentment, being mellow or being challenged and feeling exhilarated. Whilst this chapter is predominantly about positive emotions, it's useful to note that all authentic emotions have their purpose, and I'm not suggesting that it's in any way wrong to have emotions that aren't 'positive': indeed the full gamut of emotions are part of life.

There is a range of research and ideas surrounding the evolutionary purpose of emotions. One simplified approach that I find useful from psychotherapy is from Carlo Moiso (1984) who describes the natural feelings and instincts for four emotions. Figure 6.1 shows when a stimulus triggers an emotion, the feelings that ensue and the biological action and the cross-cultural or social request that is triggered in others when they witness the emotion where the emotional 'wiring' is correct. These are sometimes described as authentic emotions.

Not all emotions are authentic

Of course not everyone has the appropriate wiring in place for their emotions. Not all emotions are authentic. Even if *your* emotions are authentic, it can be useful to remember when interacting with others that their outwardly displayed emotions may not be a true representation of how they feel.

FIGURE 6.1 The feeling loop

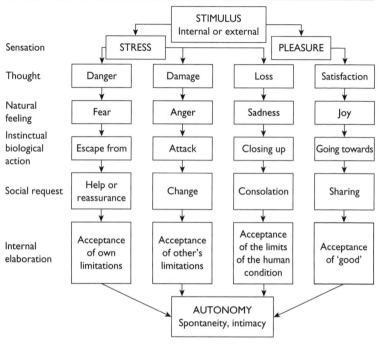

Adapted from Moiso, C (1984)

Take these two examples: firstly sometimes people get stuck for longer than necessary experiencing one particular emotion – like a car that can't get out of first gear. Alternatively sometimes the emotion can be inappropriate to the situation – more like flicking on the car indicators and instead getting jets of screen wash. In both of these examples I would describe the emotions as 'not authentic' – although the term used within transactional analysis psychotherapy is 'racket emotions' or a 'rackety display of emotion'. This inauthenticity isn't deliberate deceit, it's just sometimes people haven't been supported to develop emotional literacy.

Some of you will have had a great upbringing where a full range of emotions were supported. However many families have an unconscious taboo on a particular emotion, or on showing *any* emotion. Not surprisingly this can affect how emotions are experienced as an adult.

For example, one female CIO found that when she gets angry, instead of displaying anger, or being aware of her anger, she bursts into tears. It is relatively common for women to have this experience as it seems that when growing up it's not acceptable for little girls to be angry – so they don't always learn how to, and they subconsciously substitute emotions that are tolerable in the family environment. By contrast, little boys are often not allowed to show their fear or vulnerability – and therefore they often replace fear with another emotion such as anger or aggression.

Whilst there is a benefit in knowing about authentic emotions when working with other people, the focus for this chapter is on what you can do for yourself. You may not initially be able to tell in yourself whether an emotion is authentic, but two things can give you clues. Firstly consider if the emotion seems appropriate (in intensity and response) for the situation and secondly whether the emotion seems to last an appropriate time (often emotions are relatively fleeting, although there can be after effects).

Given that all emotions have value, I'm not suggesting that you change your authentic emotions. However, where the emotion has become 'rackety' and inauthentic then you can take action to change your mood.

It has been found that 'negative' emotions trigger a range of biological reactions within our body. Our body naturally creates additional chemicals and hormones to enhance this fight or flight response. However, in today's society we rarely have to run from sabre-toothed tigers or other predators so these chemicals in our bodies don't have a natural release through physical exertion. Over the long term a build-up of these chemicals can cause damage. Much research has taken place about the effects of negative emotions, and I certainly don't want to discount the usefulness of such emotions. However, for many of us a great day at work involves something a bit more uplifting than days filled with fear, anger and sadness.

Increasing positive authentic emotions

For many years emotions have been investigated to find their purpose and effect, but positive emotions have been largely ignored. However, recent research suggests that positive emotions *aren't the result* of success, they can *lead to* success.

Simplistically speaking, when you experience more positive emotions you'll feel good, it will have a positive impact on those around you and because emotions are contagious, it's likely to begin a virtuous circle. Feeling good might also enable you to be more creative and innovative, and enable you to see more opportunities.

What does the research say?

A researcher in the United States, Barbara Fredrickson (2009), has been exploring the purpose of positive emotions. Whereas negative emotions seem to narrow our range of responses (for example to prepare us for either flight or fight), it seems that positive emotions *broaden* our awareness, they allow us to think outside the box more. They also open our minds to different ways of doing things which can become a source of creativity. Additionally, positive emotions have been found to *build* personal resilience. Resilience is the ability to keep going when the going gets tough. Her research around positive emotions is described as the 'broaden and build' theory of positive emotions (Fredrickson, 2001).

Fredrickson (2009) found that the difference between someone who is languishing and someone who is flourishing is how many positive emotions they experience as compared to the number of negative emotions. She found that a ratio of three positive emotions to one negative emotion is the 'tipping point' in terms of thriving: people begin to thrive at ratios above 3:1. She suggests this ratio is significant, and likens the tipping point to raising the temperature of ice above zero degrees Celsius where it turns to water. It's a significant change of state that occurs.

ACTIVITY   The positivity ratio

If you are interested in accessing what your emotional ratio has been over the past 24 hours, go online and take the online questionnaire at: **www.positivityratio.com/single.php.**

The questionnaire just takes a snap-shot measure of your emotions over the past 24 hours. It can be a useful tool, especially if you're making changes and doing things which are likely to elicit more positive emotions. It can also be very interesting to see changes in your emotions over a longer time frame – recognizing that we all have off days!

If you have a more typically restrained British response to emotions, you might find the terminology of the questionnaire a little over the top – but if you can put the specific terminology to one side, I think the online survey provides useful information about your emotional level – with a great goal to aim for at least the 3:1 ratio.

Research has shown that when it comes to positive emotions, how they are generated is less important than the fact you have them. In one set of experiments (Strack *et al*, 1988) people were asked to draw a picture using their hand, mouth or foot. When holding the pen in the mouth, the pen was held in such a way it imitated a smile – at the end of the experiment those who had the false smile were happier than the other participants. When it comes to happiness, there's something to be said for faking it until you make it!

You have choice in relation to your emotions. You have probably already made the link between time perspectives and emotions. If you deliberately choose to notice positive things in the past, present or even looking forward to the future, it's likely to have an effect on your emotions.

You might be wondering how you can improve your positivity ratio and experience more positive emotions.

Experiencing positive emotions

This section has two aspects. First a caution that not all causes of positive emotions lead to an upward spiral. Then a section on developing activities to uplift you, so that you feel good and gain the health and social benefits as well as becoming increasingly resilient.

Although research shows imitating a smile can make you happier, I encourage you to be a bit picky as to where you take your positive emotions from. In the same way as your physical body needs more than calories, it needs nutrition, and not all emotions have equal 'nutritional' value. Some causes of positive emotions are the candy floss – all sugar and colourings, no nutritional value – which over time can leave a person depleted.

For example, having success at work can affect how we feel, but the downside of this is that having a rubbish day at work can also affect how we feel – and not in a good way. So if you allow your emotional life to be led by whether or not you had a great day at work you may be inadvertently depleting yourself. If the causes of 'good day' or 'bad day' are outside of your control, you're likely to feel depleted after a 'bad day', which can become a downward spiral of your emotional energy.

Let's take the straightforward example of a commission-based saleswoman. Let's assume that on her first sales call of the day, she makes the sale, and feels good. These positive emotions have her fired up, and spur her on to make the next sales call. This is great, *but* what happens when the next client is not ready for the product she's selling, and refuses the sale. She's well aware that the commission cheque would come in useful to her. How does she feel after this? Perhaps a single refusal is OK. But it's easy to predict the downward spiral if her emotions are linked to her sales performance (see Figure 6.2).

This is a mixed message. Achievement and success can be a great source of positive emotions. However, sometimes achievement can

FIGURE 6.2   Downward spiral of emotions

Negative emotions

↓

not giving off a good 'vibe'

↓

missed sales opportunity

be outside of your control. In order to build resilience, the ability to keep going when the going gets tough, have additional sources of positive emotions. Robert Kiyosaki (Kiyosaki *et al*, 1999), a successful billionaire, quotes one of his mentors by saying:

> *To be successful ... you have to be emotionally neutral to winning and losing. Winning and losing are just part of the game.*

Our emotions and moods often spill over from one aspect of our life to another. If you've had a great day at work you're likely to be in a great mood at home. In the same way, if things haven't gone well at home, it can be quite hard to contain our emotions at work. You may not notice this in yourself – often it's clearer to notice with others.

Benefits of positive emotions are that they build resilience – it's not necessary to be the equivalent of the 'laughing policeman' in your office. You can build your positive emotions in different aspects of your life and they will 'carry over' into other aspects.

Develop activities to uplift you

Experiencing positive emotions is a deliberate choice. In the same way that you can consciously adjust your time perspective, you can begin to pay attention to how you experience your emotions.

You probably already know some of the things that have an uplifting effect on you, whether it's listening to some upbeat music, looking at photos of loved ones or taking some form of physical activity.

ACTIVITY   Positive emotions

Take a moment to reflect and list some of these activities on a sheet of paper. There may be things that you only do on holiday, or things that you used to do that have fallen off the radar.

If it's true that you get what you focus on, you may as well focus on the good stuff. In Chapter 4, I encouraged you to set your vision. For how you want to live your life. Spend some time thinking about what you enjoy, and find ways to do more of it. Although the research shows that it will have a slightly detrimental effect to exclusively do the enjoyable stuff, as meaning and happiness are not found in the same activity (McGregor and Little, 1998), for most people there will still be some life chores to keep our feet on the ground.

We give energy to those things we talk about and do. What we share seems to get amplified. Therefore you can also make choices as to how you recount events to others. This is essentially the past positive time perspective I described in the previous chapter.

I used to envy the friends who always seemed to have such a good time. They might be doing much the same things as I did ... but where I found the things I did always ordinary and mainly dull, these friends were always involved in events which were interesting and exciting. It took me years to realize that the differences between these friends and me was not in what we did, or what we felt about what we did, but how we talked about what we did.

Rowe (1988)

However, experiencing more positive emotions is more than just a matter of changing our attention to notice the good and hyping up our experiences! What follows are five suggestions for activities that you can carry out, which have supporting research and are therefore likely to increase your daily amount of positive emotions (see Figure 6.3):

1 Gratitude/three good things.
2 Acts of kindness.

FIGURE 6.3 Ways to develop positive emotions

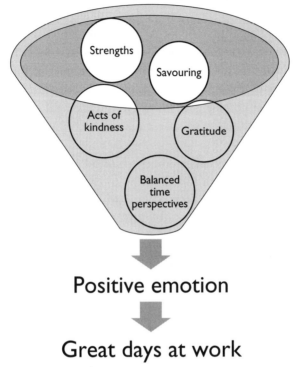

Positive emotion

Great days at work

Adapted from Hazelton, 2012

3 Savouring (Chapter 5).

4 Strengths (Chapter 9).

5 Balanced time perspectives (Chapter 5).

Gratitude

A daily dose of gratitude is important for our well-being. Gratitude is about being thankful. Often within our work day we have many 'to-dos': projects to start, actions to take, and people to meet. I acknowledge that work can sometimes be downright frustrating and our behaviours can become driven or obsessive – and that's before we get home. Sometimes in the rush to do the next thing we can lose sight of what we've done, what we've achieved and, more importantly, what we're thankful for.

Find a way of acknowledging what you're grateful for in a way that suits you. Some people share this activity with family over dinner. Other people use a daily personal gratitude journal where they record what they're grateful for. Another suggestion is a clear cookie jar where you write your daily gratitude notes on coloured pieces of paper, which can quickly become a visual reminder of the good in life – especially helpful if you occasionally experience days when it just seems that nothing goes the way you'd planned!

Acts of kindness

This is about finding opportunities to spread a little kindness, and not necessarily through formal giving to charity. This could be to work colleagues, friends or strangers; acts of kindness can also be welcomed at home (Lyubomirsky, 2010).

Experiment with different activities in different contexts: pay a compliment about the quality of work, assist someone with their bags or a buggy, give *cash* to charity, volunteer your *time* to a charity or to a local community cause, etc.

It's important not to expect anything in return when you're giving your random act of kindness. As the giver you will experience a warm 'feel good' glow. It's been found that if you do several different acts of kindness in one day, it has a bigger impact than if 'kindness' becomes routine. In the same way that many of us get used to a pay increase rather too quickly, we also get used to the 'feel good glow' which is generated from acts of kindness. If we adopt a 'good deed of the day' approach it's likely not to be as effective as if we do three deeds one day, and none the next. Keep your acts of kindness fresh by mixing up what you do, where you do it and who you do it with.

Savouring

Savouring can be done for each of the time perspectives. You can look forward to something happening in the future in anticipation.

In the now, you can enjoy the experience. Mentally slow it down, notice the sights, sounds, smells and your feelings.

Looking back, having had the experience, you can then revisit it – ideally quite soon after the event to reinforce your memories. You can simply remember it alone. However, one alternative that I recommend is to savour with a buddy who understands savouring – you will find the experience becomes amplified.

Strengths

We often overlook what comes easy to us, but this is usually what can make us successful if we're aware of it and know how to harness it. Finding your strengths and finding new ways to use them, and harnessing them in times of crisis can provide you with a range of positive emotions, from a sense of calm to a real buzz. Strengths are covered more in Chapter 9.

Balanced time perspective

Having a balanced time perspective is also a useful way of developing your positive emotions. Know when to look back and savour and reminisce, have goals and strive for them, and be aware and make a choice in the moment. Time perspectives were covered more fully in Chapter 5, and goal setting is covered in Chapter 7.

You have activities that you already do, activities that uplift you that you know about but may have fallen off your radar, and now you have some additional suggestions around savouring, gratitude and acts of kindness. Doing these activities on a regular basis will build your resilience.

When our mood dips, it's not always easy to remember to do something uplifting. My suggestion is that you develop your plan when you're upbeat. Put it in place for easy access when you need it. Often when our mood sinks so does our motivation – so it almost has to be easier to carry out the steps on the plan than not.

Whilst you're feeling upbeat, you may know that a long walk in the park has an uplifting effect on you. However, when our mood dips this can seem 'too much'. Create a plan with small underwhelming steps. Perhaps a walk to the canteen or to the postbox is enough to begin to change your emotional state. The next chapter looks at goals – and the importance of small and sometimes underwhelming goals to make progress.

Summary

- A range of emotions is part of the human condition.

- All emotions have a purpose; however for convenience these are labelled 'positive' and 'negative' emotions, which might undermine the value from so-called negative emotions.

- Not all emotions are authentic.

- Positive emotions are good for you, and good for those around you.

- Positive emotions build resilience and broaden our outlook and ability to see opportunities.

- Research has shown that negative emotions have more impact than positive ones – so we need more positive emotions to counter the negative.

- There are ways to increase your daily experience of positive emotions.

More information

If you want to track your emotions, there is an app for the iPhone at: **http://www.mappiness.org.uk/**

7
Goals – the engine room powering success

Goals provide an important 'how to' in terms of achieving your vision. Goals are things that you want to achieve. By definition, they are something that you want in the future, so they also are a manifestation of the future time orientation.

The corporate world is full of 'vision, objectives, goals, measures etc' but what does this mean and how does it really relate to helping us achieve our personal and professional outcomes? The first thing is that a goal can be large or small; it is something that you are focused on achieving, be it a promotion, a new job, or winning an achievement award – all the way to taking your idea and becoming the next Google or Facebook. In essence a goal is something that you want to become or achieve.

Constantly achieving small goals can help to keep you motivated on a day-to-day basis. I've noticed that many people have difficulty in setting goals for themselves and therefore I think the goals theme warrants its own chapter.

If you're the type of person who already regularly sets and reviews their goals then congratulations – you're in the minority. Feel free to use this chapter as a refresher. Unfortunately, I've found that many people find setting and achieving goals something that is hard to do. For some people it can be a deeper issue, but for most of us it's not knowing where to start – with the intention of doing it 'later' – and then 'life' gets in the way.

Some goals are imposed upon us. Until we can find a way to make these imposed goals our own, they are typically not motivating, and they just become 'more stuff' that we have to do. Goals that are imposed can work in the short term – after all they are added to our 'to-do' list. And there's typically someone holding us accountable to ensure they get done. However, for longer-term sustained success, and for your personal goals, you have to take ownership, and that generally means you have to set some goals for yourself.

The reason that it's important to 'own' your goals is that this is where your intrinsic motivation comes from. You may remember from Chapter 4 that intrinsic motivation is a generator and power-house of energy, and as such is hugely important in our success.

Whilst our motivation seems highly complex, in my opinion it can be boiled down into four steps which form the basis of 4MAT learning theory (see page 231). (McCarthy and O'Neill-Blackwell, 2007).

Goal setting

For every goal that we set we need to know 'why' we're doing it. How does it fit into our vision or form part of our life purpose? Once we're clear on why we're doing something, it is then useful to be really clear on 'what' we are going to do: then, 'how' it's going to be done, anticipating the way round obstacles anticipating the 'if'.

In defining what needs to be done, setting SMART goals – Specific, Measurable, Achievable, Realistic and Timebound – can be a useful way to ensure that we don't get too carried away by over engineering something (see also page 154). We need to set SMART goals to be clear about what standard we're going to aim for.

Most goals don't require 'excellence', they require regular and consistent activity. However, I notice that some people don't start unless they can do an excellent job. Excellence comes through sustained effort and practice. Andy Murray didn't wake up a British tennis champion; it took years of hard work and practice. Similarly Alan Sugar, Bill Gates and Steve Jobs didn't spring from nowhere, but their success and fame came from years of hard work and balanced risk taking. Be clear on what your desired outcome is and take some time to think through the implications: how will it affect you and others as you strive for, and eventually achieve, your goal? Consider this before you start, because when you commit to do something – really commit. You already know there will be dips in your motivation, so don't allow yourself excuses to give up on yourself.

So, you know why you're doing something, what you're going to do, and you've got some clear goals. The next section considers how you will achieve your task. Let's take the simplified example of a presentation.

Jenny wanted a promotion at work. She knew that her new role would require her to present at team meetings, something that she wasn't comfortable doing. However, Jenny decided that because the promotion was important to her longer-term vision, she would invest the time and energy in learning to present. Jenny had her 'why'.

She agreed with her manager that she would give a 10-minute presentation at the team meeting in March. The outcome of the presentation would be to enlist her co-team members to assist her with some testing. In having this agreement, she knew clearly 'what' she was going to do, and the goal was well on the way to becoming SMART.

However, having clarity on what the goal was didn't help Jenny with 'how' she would achieve it. She needed to develop an action plan, to find some training, create the presentation and practise it.

As a final step, she needed to think about some of the obstacles, some of the 'what if' scenarios, and ensure that she had some plans to cope. Fortunately, Jenny wasn't one to start catastrophizing, but it's always useful to re-connect with our motivation for achieving goals, because sometimes the goal itself may not be inherently motivating – it's a means to an end.

As I've described it above, working towards the goal is devoid of feedback, but if Jenny had an action plan she could see how well she was doing against the plan. Hopefully her presentation practice would be with someone experienced in presentations who could provide some constructive comments as well as much encouragement. We all need feedback.

Consider what constitutes feedback for you. How will you know that you're making progress towards your goals? How will you know that what you're doing is working? No system works in isolation, you also need the ability to monitor and to make adjustments.

SMART goals

Often what we're passionate about becomes our vision. Our goals then become the milestones we want to achieve along the way. There is much written about SMART goals, the importance of having goals that are:

- Specific;
- Measurable;
- Achievable;
- Realistic;
- Timebound.

I've seen slight variances on the words used, but typically the essence is similar.

Often we set goals that aren't SMART. You might set yourself the goal of having 'a great day at work', but it does not meet all of the criteria for it being a SMART goal. Here are some questions you could begin to ask yourself to turn 'a great day at work' into a smart goal:

- How could you make it more specific? For example, what does 'great' in a great day at work mean to you?
- How will you measure your success?

ACTIVITY   Goals part II

This is a continuation of the activity in Chapter 4, and is designed to further clarify some of your personal goals. Set aside approximately 10 minutes. You will need sheets of paper (suggest A4 or larger), a pencil or pen and a timer. There are no 'right' answers to this exercise. The purpose of this activity is to help you identify and clarify what *you* want.

1   Take a sheet and write at the top: **What do I want to achieve in the next three years?**

    - Write down as many ideas as you can in two minutes exactly.
    - Then take another two minutes to review, alter or add.

2   Take another sheet and write at the top: **If I knew I would be struck dead by lightning six months from today, how would I live until then?**

    - Take exactly two minutes to brainstorm with yourself on this question.
    - Then another two minutes to review, alter or add. (Assume that all arrangements for your funeral etc have already been dealt with.)

3   Now spend *at least* another two minutes reviewing the entire set of answers on all three (including the sheet from Chapter 4) of your sheets together. This stage is not timed, and you can spend as long on it as you want. Again you can use this chance to refine, add or subtract from your overall list on all three sheets so that it becomes even more satisfying to you.

4   It is important to express all your goals in *positive* words – that is, in terms of what you *will* do, get or achieve. If you have worded any of your goals in negative terms – what you *will not do* or *stop* doing, or *avoid* then see if you can also write it in a positive way. Ask yourself: 'What am I going to have, or do *instead* of ...'

5   Consider whether there are sharp differences between your lifetime, three-year and six-month lists. If so, does this tell you anything about what you really want from life? Typically the six-month list contains more pleasures – and it can be useful to consider your balance between long term and short term.

    Once again make any refinements to your combined list, taking as much time as you like.

6 Look for *conflicts* between goals on any one list and between lists. You should regard conflicts as a positive aspect of your lists because having identified them, you've also registered the need to deal with them. Conflicts between goals can be dealt with in either or both of two ways:

   a Setting priorities.

   b Refinement and adaption.

7 Now take a fourth piece of paper, and label it: **My priority goals for the coming year.** Look at all three of the lists you have already. Keep potential conflicts in mind as you do this. Considering all the goals you have listed on the other three lists, now choose six priority goals that you are going to achieve **in the coming twelve months**.

In order to get realistic twelve-month goals, you may have to take priority goals from your lifetime or three-year lists and translate them into 'twelve-month' versions. For example, if one of your three-year goals is to 'run a mile in under five minutes' the corresponding twelve-month goal might be to 'run a mile in under six minutes'.

In a business context it could be that in five years you want to be running a division, or to have achieved a certain percentage market share. It is then necessary to work out the key targets that must be met in the interim to achieve that goal. I suggest getting really clear on what must be done in the first twelve months. Look for key milestones, skills that you need to acquire, things you need to learn, behaviours that you must change, people you must get acquainted / network with. The clearer you are on the intermediate steps and the actions you must take to achieve those steps (or mini goals) the more direct your progress will be.

You should have some daily targets and activities that when completed will add up and take you to your goal. The good thing about five-year or more planning is that at the outset you don't need all the details; you can't predict the future and what might happen between now and then, but if you are heading in the right direction you are moving forward! You can always change direction as new information or situations change, but you will have achieved so much more along the way than if you just drift through like a rudderless ship on the tides of life.

8 Review your goals regularly. These goals are not 'etched in stone'. In fact, especially in the early stages of goal setting, you will benefit from reviewing and re-working the lists through several drafts. Effective goals are not static, but are constantly subject to revision.

In addition to having a long-term vision, remember I strongly advocate setting near-term underwhelming goals. There is huge satisfaction and personal reward to be had in completing a task and moving on to the next. The very act of achieving something motivates you to do more. When you create small achievements it provides the fuel for the next burst of activity. There's also something about leaving something undone – the brain doesn't like something unfinished – so a tip is to leave a task when you are still raring to go. It means you are more likely to come back to it – and achieve it ... and start the next.

Clear goals along with an action plan and some key performance measures along the way will have you accelerating towards your vision in no time. They will help you stay the course and overcome the natural challenges you will face along the way. In the next chapter we will take a closer look at healthy work habits that you can employ to propel your career or business forward.

Summary

- Goals are the 'how to' for achieving your vision.
- Have your five-year plan for work, and set twelve-month goals.
- Divide twelve-month goals into clear quarterly specific actions that are under your control – use SMART to assist you with this.
- Know what to achieve on a weekly or daily basis.
- Keep daily targets 'underwhelming' as you are more likely to consistently achieve them even when they don't seem like a priority.

8
Working habits – creating habits that support you

We are what we repeatedly do. Excellence, then, is not an act, but a habit.

Aristotle

You may have already decided that you want to make some changes to your days, or perhaps you've spotted some new things that you want to try. Perhaps you want to be a little more mindful; enjoy some more savouring; or be really focused and make progress towards your goals. Doing an activity once is easy enough, but 'once' doesn't make it a habit. For many of us changing a habit can be a slightly longer process. Lyubomirsky (2010) describes behaviours as habitual 'when you don't have to make the decision to do them'.

In order to achieve real success and have great days at work two skills are important: firstly the ability to consciously be aware of, and have the desire to change, our habits; and secondly the power of decision making. Habits by their very nature are ingrained behaviours – they are short cuts we have developed. However, a habit that has been formed can also be changed! All it takes is a little time, an ample measure of motivation, and a good dose of discipline to follow through. Once you have decided to change, expect to have to cope with a sprinkling of frustration along the way. It might sound pretty tough but when you really want to succeed, anything is possible.

You already know that there's no magic formula for changing habits – the big shift has to come from within for change to be lasting. *You have to be motivated to change.* Pink (2009), quoting the work of Deci from 1955 describes how it is 'wrong to think that motivation is something that gets done to people rather than something that people do'. Motivation is the power source of change, and it comes from within us.

The good news is that you can change your habits. Having a clear 'towards' vision will sustain you through the process, along with adopting an 'I can' growth mindset. In all probability you may experience some setbacks along the way, but forewarned is forearmed. While some people allow setbacks to get in the way of forming a new habit remember that a setback is not failure. How to handle setbacks is further discussed under the heading of 'bounce back' in Chapter 9. Both of these combine to enable you to continue to make progress towards your new habit.

How do you know what to change? When thinking about habits, there are probably some trivial things that we currently pay attention to, which takes effort to make decisions about. It's often beneficial to automate these things. Conversely there are other aspects of our life that we currently do automatically and which, if we were to switch and 'pay attention' to, would lead us to more great days at work. In order to understand this process better, here are some examples.

Automate these things

Having written about the importance of cultivating mindfulness (in Chapter 5), of doing things with conscious awareness, it seems that the opposite is also true – by that I mean the automation of doing some things without conscious awareness. Decision making does take energy. Remember when you first started to drive a car? Do you recall how tired you were at the end of an hour's lesson as compared to now, when those skills are second nature? Therefore, it's useful to design our routines to automate activities either that you want to cultivate or that you don't want to waste your prime consciousness thinking about.

What do you currently deliberate about? These can be really small things, for example deciding what to do next, when to make the call to the client, when to check for e-mail (again) – or even whether to respond as you notice the new alert – and of course whether to have another cup of coffee now, or after the next task. Each of these small decisions saps our energy. These are the things that you need to automate, or have a process in place as much as possible so that you don't waste your thinking on 'Shall I make calls first or check e-mail?' Don't use your prime thinking capacity on insignificant decisions.

Having a clear plan of action prepared the night before means that you don't have to waste time and energy 'getting down to work' when you arrive in work. It also means that when you do get disrupted or interrupted by a colleague or client you can quickly get back to doing what you were doing before. Also by preparing an action list the night before enables your brain to work on any problems etc in your sleep. This is especially powerful if you are involved in creative problem solving since it enables a different part of your mind to work.

Don't be surprised if in the morning while you are in 'neutral', say brushing your teeth or in the shower, the solution pops into your mind. An action list is a way to automate on a micro-level, and you can change the automation each day to suit requirements. If you find yourself doing the same things every day then it might be good to put some of these things in your diary as 'tasks', ie at 9 am every day you check the server logs and then check e-mail and voicemail.

It's been noted that several successful men and women have limited their choices in aspects of their life that are unimportant to them. One aspect to this is about creating habits that make it easier to do something than not. For example, many people talk about the routine of getting up and doing a form of exercise. They create an environment that makes it easy, and reduces their decisions, automating the process to help them to form the habit. For example, laying out running gear the night before and setting the alarm with an underwhelming goal of making it out the front door.

Automating your routine decisions and activities means that you don't use your mental processing power on the small stuff. This means you can focus your attention on what's important to you. When you achieve what's important to you, it will contribute to you experiencing great days at work.

What does the research say?

Automating things is likely to lead to achievement. The research on achievement and mastery is compelling, for health and well-being (Roepke and Grant, 2011).

Additionally, the research shows that constant small decisions wear us down – when we repeatedly have to make the (same) decision. Wansink *et al* (2006) experimented with how the distance from and visibility of sweets on the desks of secretaries affected how many they ate. They moved the bowls to be either in reach or out of reach, and they also changed the bowls from being clear glass to opaque. Then over four weeks they noted how many sweets were eaten on a daily basis (see Figure 8.1).

Tony Schwartz (2010), quoting the work of Wansink and Painter, commented on the link between the number of decisions and self-regulation:

> We can turn the candy down once ... but when the candy is on the desk in front of us, then we're making a 'no' decision every 5 minutes, and over time it becomes harder to say no, and maintain motivation towards a goal of weight regulation.

Take a moment to consider: what are some of the low-value activities that you currently spend time thinking and changing your mind

FIGURE 8.1 Number of sweets consumed

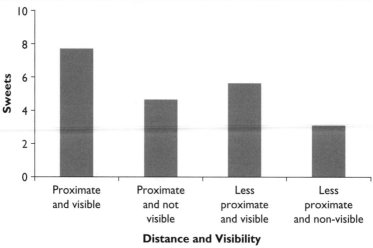

Adapted from Wansink, 2006

about? What measures can you put in place so that you don't have to continually decide? Putting routines in place, in the short term, can feel like lack of choice (and ultimately you do have the choice to adapt or even scrap your routine) – but over the longer term, the ultimate satisfaction of achieving more will be well worth it. Suggestions for automating some of your work tasks include creating a default diary or a perpetual to-do list which gives a structure for the activities and releases your mental capacity.

With your routine tasks automated, you will have more thinking and decision-making capacity to focus on your strategic activities, as well as creative energy to focus on innovations. When you make a conscious decision to take a step back, you may notice additional tasks which you may be able to delegate, or realize that they are not adding value, and stop them.

Paying attention or focus

Earlier we looked at the process of learning – which was a series of steps. At the highest level 'unconscious competence' is automatic behaviour. As with many things if you completely 'automate' there is the danger that bad habits will creep in, or that the environment will subtly change and you will either no longer be at peak performance or what you are doing will no longer be totally relevant.

Therefore, it is important that when you have reached 'unconscious competence' there must be an active process of review and self-assessment or at the very least some form of attention if you are to maintain peak performance. The challenge is that when you become so competent at something and have automated an activity or thought process then you need to self-assess. This is where peer review and 360-degree assessments can prove invaluable. For some of the things you do automatically, flick the switch and do them with more conscious awareness (conscious competence). For example, your thoughts occur, but most people don't explore what's going on – whether thoughts are useful or self-sabotaging.

In order to further develop your ability to have great days at work I suggest for at least part of the day you 'pay attention' to your thoughts, noticing whether you're approaching a situation from either a growth or fixed mindset. Approach your thoughts with curiosity. Some people berate themselves when they notice that they have a fixed mindset but it doesn't help to verbally 'beat yourself up'. Just choose to notice your thinking with a light and breezy curiosity, for example, 'Oh that's interesting. I seem to be thinking I can't do a good job on the presentation next week ...' and you could add '... and how could I think about it differently or do something different?'

Doing something differently is essentially learning new behaviours, which was described in Chapter 2. Remember when you're in the middle stages your learning might feel clunky or frustrating – and that's OK – you're learning; be kind to yourself. Seth Godin wrote a great book (*The Dip*, 2007) about the feelings of frustration that occur in the middle of any project. The dip is a crucial point when you need to make an active decision to continue on and 'push through the wall'. If you give up at that point you will never know the success you could have achieved. Judging whether you are simply 'in the dip' or have hit a real dead end can be challenging. (To learn more about this I highly recommend Seth's excellent book.)

Your 'automatic' or habitual thoughts can either focus on the negative in life, or on the positive. Sometimes our thinking patterns don't serve us. A particular form of thought pattern is our beliefs. Beliefs are the things that we hold to be true. One example is a child's belief in Santa Claus. Many of our beliefs get updated as we get older, but if we have beliefs that don't get updated, they can hold us back. For example, one such belief in childhood – and for very good reasons – was being told 'Don't talk to strangers.' This can become unconsciously ingrained in a person's being, and cause them to be reluctant to initiate conversations with people they don't know, perhaps at a networking event, or a kick-off meeting with people from other departments.

Our beliefs generally cause us to look for supporting evidence – and then we essentially ignore any contrary evidence. For example, imagine a person who has a fixed mindset about the quality of their work. They look for all the evidence that their work is great – but every time they hear anything that runs counter to their view, they might blame the other person for not understanding or become defensive. Perhaps in the short term this means that the person doesn't have to make any change – until a manager is forced to initiate some form of personal improvement plan.

Belief change

One approach to changing beliefs has been developed from the field of Cognitive Behavioural Therapy (CBT). It's based on the work of Dr Aaron Beck, and is described more fully in *The Resilience Factor* (Reivich and Shatté, 2002) and *Life Coaching* (Neenan and Dryden, 2002). It involves knowing your ABCs:

- A – Activating event;
- B – Belief;
- C – Consequences (emotional and behavioural).

Often we think that the activating event triggers our emotions and behaviours ie A to C: however, this is typically not the case, it's the belief that we hold. For example:

A – Activating event: Jane's boss gives her some feedback around the quality of a document.

C – Consequence: As a consequence Jane feels her eyes welling up with tears. However, it's not the feedback which causes the tears, it's what Jane tells herself, her belief that upsets her.

B – Belief: If Jane believes that she must do a perfect job at all times then there will always be opportunity for her to be disappointed with herself. She may begin to catastrophize that this piece of feedback signals the beginning of a disciplinary hearing, which will result in her losing her job, house etc.

Finding the belief can sometimes look easy, and sometimes it is. When you catch yourself using compulsory language like 'should' and 'must', you can explore what you believe to be true. Once you've discovered the belief, in the ABC model you can move to your Ds and Es where D stands for Dispute and E for Effective new approach.

D – Dispute: You can dispute the belief in a number of different ways. You can challenge the existing belief with the question 'Really?' For example, 'Really? Is a single piece of constructive feedback likely to result in the loss of a job? Some minor spelling mistakes and poor formatting in a single document whilst being slightly careless does not make it likely that I'll lose my job.'

The next step is to see if holding a different belief would support you better.

Take this example: you're sitting at lunch in the canteen, you notice some people a couple of tables away pointing in your direction and you think you overhear your name being mentioned and some light laughter. What do you think?

Many years ago Adam, a work colleague, described making an active choice around social chit-chat at work. If he thought people were talking about him in insignificant situations, he said: 'If there is a good thing or a bad thing to think, I choose the good'. When taken to an extreme, this behaviour could be delusional, but it proved effective for day-to-day living, and helped keep my colleague in good cheer!

E – Effective new approach to the problem: Approaches which change how you think about something, and affect what you do are some of the most useful tools there are to help you feel better about life. Some of the positive psychology interventions are a great way of changing habits, for example making a note of three good things every day, starts to 're-program' the brain to notice the good things.

Decision making

When we have successfully automated our routine activities, more of our prime thinking capacity is freed up for more important decisions.

In Chapter 3, I suggested that too much choice wasn't good for us. This suggestion is supported by research. Professor Peterson (2006), describing the work of Barry Schwartz, suggests that as the number of options we have increases, so does the amount of time we spend making decisions *plus* we experience more regret. Barry Schwartz noted that over the years his choice had increased in buying jeans. From the limited range of makes and styles of yesteryear, to the huge number available today, including different colours, shades and fits. He noted that after making the decision he fretted about making the right choice. Simply put, having so many options increases the opportunity for 'post-purchase dissonance' – that is the self-questioning 'Did I make the right and best choice?' People are by nature either satisficers or maximizers.

As we saw earlier taking a decision is usually better than taking no decision even though in today's over-optioned society that can be hard! A pair of new jeans is better than no jeans, but how long do we spend choosing the jeans ... do we go for the 'best' or simply 'good enough'? There are often consequences when no decision is reached – and what about the different ways people actively make decisions? Broadly speaking people tend to make decisions in one of two ways. The academic literature refers to these decision making strategies as maximizing and satisfying. Most of us will have a preference for one or the other strategy and they might be different in different contexts.

Maximizers want to make the very best choice among alternatives, whereas satisficers are those that are content to make a good-enough choice. Of course we are typically neither fully one nor the other. I know my tendency is to want to consider all the options thoroughly before making a decision, which would make me more of a maximizer. However, I also have lots of experience of making quick decisions.

Several years ago I wanted to buy a digital camera prior to a business trip to South Africa. I have a friend who had recently bought a camera and I called her up and asked her what I should look for. She said that the camera should have a viewfinder as well as a screen for bright conditions. When I visited the store I gave my criteria to the sales assistant who had just one camera with a viewfinder and screen – and, I think much to her surprise, I bought it.

In business we're often encouraged to do 'due diligence' prior to business decision making, which can slow things down and encourage a maximizing decision-making strategy. This can be where larger organizations with more formal processes lose out to smaller and more agile organizations which make 'satisficing' and 'good enough' decisions. On a personal note, it's interesting to note that maximizers take longer to arrive at a decision, and they experience less satisfaction with their decision. This remains true even if the final decision seems better than the quicker decisions made by satisficers. The lesson seems to be, make quick decisions and move on.

However you make decisions, be sure to make them if you want to have great days at work and progress your career. Often the most damaging choice to your mental health is the decision you didn't take, and the opportunity that slipped away.

Summary

- Some habits regarding how you think need to be disrupted to ensure they're not holding you back. Other actions during your day you'll benefit from automating.
- Taking decisions takes energy – prioritize big decisions.
- Whilst automating what you do, and following a checklist, may seem dull, the benefits are twofold: it ensures that things get done consistently and it frees our brains for more creative output in other areas.
- Look for opportunities to use a 'satisficing' or good enough decision-making strategy.

9
Self-mastery – maximizing your well-being and overcoming obstacles

This chapter is broadly split into two sections. Firstly there are some important physiological aspects relating to our well-being. *Physiology* refers to all aspects of our mechanical and physical self along with the biochemical functions of our organs. Within the context of great days at work, I discuss patterns of sleep, nutrition and exercise. The second section of this chapter is about increasing our personal awareness, understanding our strengths and being aware of some tools to deal with the inevitable obstacles in life.

A great number of people will benefit from starting with self-mastery. In my experience if someone's lacking confidence, then the 'self-mastery' column is the place to start as it develops awareness of existing areas of mastery as well as introducing new ones.

Physiology

Much of this book has been about addressing your thoughts: for example, what you think, how you think, and how you might change what you think if you choose. Although we've looked at emotions, until now we haven't explored how our physical body can influence our mental happiness.

The body has some essential needs around nutrition, water, exercise and sleep. In order to have more great days at work there may be some small (or large) adjustments that you could make in any one of these areas which would lead you to have more great days at work.

ACTIVITY   Your health

How do you currently look after your body?

_____

_____

What else could you do?

_____

_____

These questions are deliberately vague. For most people they know the answer to 'what they could do'; the stumbling block is translating their plans into actions.

Most people know what they 'should' do, in order to make improvements in these areas. The importance of good nutrition is well documented, it is not 'new news' and the refrain 'you are what you eat' is now familiar. Most people understand that food is fuel for your body, and therefore if you eat low-grade food, then it's not surprising that your energy may not be of a high quality.

Another aspect of nutrition is water, and there is also much documented evidence that most people typically don't drink enough water. Studies have found that a 5 per cent increase in our hydration can lead to a 20 per cent increase in performance.

How do we know if we're fully hydrated? The signs of dehydration are easier to spot – dry lips, thirst and darker coloured urine. Although thirst is a sign of dehydration many of us confuse the 'thirst' signal from our body and think we're hungry – so then we eat rather than drink.

You know what to do. Eat good food; little and often. For most of us, increase the amount of fruit and vegetables in our diet and drink more water – up to 2.5 litres per day for men and 2 litres for women. If you want to make changes, set some V-SUC goals.

Ensure the goals you set are connected to your vision, ensure they are the right size (start with underwhelming goals that give you the feel-good factor when you successfully complete them) and that you can cross them off your list. Nutrition and water are not discussed further, but briefly I'll explore more of the research around sleep and physical activity.

Sleep

It's important to get a good night's sleep. OK, this is obvious, right? You know that when you do sleep well, you feel better. We all know the results of a missed night's sleep, either from 'an all-nighter' from student days or in order to complete a project, or even as a result of jet lag.

However, something called 'sleep debt' can build up over a longer period of time. Dr William Dement (Dement and Vaughan, 2000) suggests that the brain keeps 'an exact accounting of how much sleep is owed'. The less sleep you get, the more in debt to sleep you are, and the more sleepy you become. The debt has to be repaid – or results in sleepiness. Sleep deprivation has been cited as a cause of several high-profile accidents such as the Exxon Valdez disaster and the NASA Challenger disaster. Post-event analysis showed that sleep deprivation was attributed as a cause in both accidents, although it is a contributory cause in countless other smaller, and yet tragic accidents, as well as mundane errors of judgement.

It seems that sleep debt and alcohol are uncomfortable bedfellows, with sleepiness increasing the impact of alcohol.

Before describing in more detail some of the biological benefits of having good sleep I recognize that sometimes we don't get a good night's sleep. I can't change that you may have a disturbed night's sleep, whether from worry, children or noisy neighbours, but you can do a lot to maximize the chances of falling asleep quickly. You can do this by adopting good sleep habits – developing a regular 'ritual' or routine for going to bed.

It's wise to keep the TV and laptop out of the bedroom, and if you do experience problems sleeping, don't watch it before going to sleep as it can overstimulate your brain. If you have trouble falling asleep, notice what you watch before bedtime (whether in the bedroom or not). The news can have disturbing elements which can set your mind racing when what's needed is something more calming.

Good sleep hygiene also means excluding caffeine for several hours before sleeping. Eat at least three hours before bed, which gives your body time to have digested most of your meal. If you find you wake up in the night with lots of ideas, keep a notebook by the bed to jot your thoughts down – this means you can go back to sleep safe in the knowledge that you'll remember your ideas. If you find that you either can't sleep because of worry, or wake up with worry then allocate some 'worry time' earlier in the evening. Research has shown that it's also useful to keep a gratitude diary. Before bed, take a moment to 'savour' the events of the day – a bit of past positive reflection.

What happens when we're asleep is more than the body shutting down. There are some biological processes that only take place when you're asleep. These processes help to create a healthy immune system and are good for reducing stress levels.

Good sleep has been firmly linked to good health. Mild sleep deprivation can make people irritable; and at the extreme, sleep deprivation is a form of torture. Feeling and being healthy are important aspects to pay attention to if you want more great days at work. You don't have to increase the amount of sleep you get by *hours* to experience the benefits. Experiment with getting an extra 20 minutes of sleep per night. Perhaps automating some of your routines will make you more efficient in the morning; alternatively skip the late night news, decide not to check e-mails before bed and retire to bed just 20 minutes earlier.

Micro-rests

For most of us, taking a nap at work is not really the 'done thing', and most organizations don't have napping facilities. There are of course exceptions and forward-thinking organizations such as Google, Cisco, Apple and Pixar encourage napping (Schwartz *et al*, 2010). This can be to minimize the increased risks of accident associated with excessive drowsiness, and it also can be for enhanced productivity.

While research into napping is still in its infancy, it has begun to show through objective measures that napping is effective. However, on waking from a nap the person often *feels* groggy and less effective. Most people have experienced an afternoon nap, but you may want to conduct your own experiment. Note how you feel before a nap and then post-nap see what effect it has on you and your productivity for the rest of the day.

Although it is not technically sleep, what I'll explore next is a 90-second rest through breathing. When Jim Loehr (Loehr and Schwartz, 2003) was coaching world-class tennis players, he studied videos of the very best players. He noticed that the difference at the very top levels of the game seemed to be not how they won their points but how the players micro-recovered *between* points. I use the analogy of it being like the full stops in sentences. Not large, but they help to make the sentences have meaning.

In Chapter 5 I described mindful meditation – here's a different approach around breathing. It only takes 90 seconds – and you can do it at your desk.

Through my yoga practice, and having spent some time learning how to meditate, I've become increasingly aware of the importance of focused breathing. Over the years I've regularly practised deep breathing as a way of staying calm or calming down. The benefits from breathing were considered as a bit 'new age', until some research found how breathing affects the heart. A company called HeartMath developed a programme of 'controlled breathing and positive thinking' as a stress-busting activity. What the yogis have known for several millennia now has 'science' to back it up.

You can focus on your breathing standing or sitting. The breathing should be deep but not laboured, ie it should feel natural and not forced. You will know if it is comfortable. HeartMath suggest breathing out for a count of five and in for a count of five, but if that's too much for you, do less. HeartMath also suggest simultaneously focusing on a past enjoyable experience.

Notice how you feel before you start; now give it a go.

ACTIVITY   Controlled breathing

Breathe in for a count of five, and out for a count of five. Do that for 90 seconds ... or nine full cycles which I find easier than clock watching, but a gentle alarm works well too.

And breathe.

Notice how you feel now.

HeartMath suggest using their technique at intervals throughout the day from these micro rests, let's now take a look at something more active.

Physical activity

Whether or not you participate in regular physical activity, you know that exercise is good for you. But you may not realize just how far-reaching the research is – or the breadth of activities that contribute to physical activity. The International Physical Activity Questionnaire (IPAQ) is a short questionnaire you can use to determine your current level of physical activity.

https://docs.google.com/viewer?a=v&pid=sites&srcid=ZGVmYXVsd GRvbWFpbnx0aGVpcGFxfGd4OjhlMTcxZGJkZmMxYTg1NQ

For more information, and questionnaires in a language other than English: **https://sites.google.com/site/theipaq/**

The recommended guidance is 30 minutes per day of physical activity (Biddle and Mutrie, 2001). The evidence around exercise is compelling. There are studies citing links between physical activity and many positive effects. One of the most influential is the study indicating exercise is better than drugs, specifically the use of antidepressants (Babyak *et al*, 2000).

> A while ago, I realized that unless I made a positive choice to do some form of exercise, my lifestyle would remain relatively inactive. One thing I have personally found useful is to track my activity. I started record-keeping – which helps form a positive feedback loop.

There are many ways to keep records of your activity, from simply marking a calendar, to GPS-enabled logging on a smartphone. Whatever you choose, simply seeing a record of what you've done can spur you on to do more. Whether or not you participate in regular physical activity, you're probably aware of the benefits and importance to your health. The next section is about how our genetic make-up can impact our well-being, which may not be so well known.

Genetics... *well some of it is*

In reading about how to have more great days at work, some people may think 'but I'm just not wired that way'. Or you may have come across people who say 'that's just the way I am', and to some extent that is true. In addition to our thoughts being able to limit us, our genetic wiring comes into play. Our genetic make-up forms about 40 per cent of our happiness levels so we are capable of change. However, happiness is not the same as something like eye colour, which is 'given' and unchangeable.

Even if someone didn't have *any* genetic predisposition towards happiness and well-being, through their own additional efforts they can still affect up to 60 per cent of their well-being. I hope by now that you've seen you can influence and change a significant amount of what you might have thought were 'givens', which can increase the likelihood of having great days at work.

You may not care about your genetic predisposition towards happiness. In fact being 'happy' and improving your 'well-being' may not be at the top of this week's 'to-do' list. You may have other goals and challenges – you may want the next promotion, or successful completion of your project. However what I've found is that for most professionals 'happiness' underlies their immediate 'wants'.

I have worked with many business professionals to help them understand their underlying values. With their permission, I repeatedly ask an annoying question: 'And if you get that (whatever "that" is), what will it mean to you?' Despite its slightly pompous name, 'values elicitation' is a very powerful tool which digs deep to uncover what is important to us and what drives and guides us. You can try it for yourself to find what your core or underlying values are.

For many of us happiness forms one of those underlying values – but don't let that influence your answers! Here's an example just so you can see how repetitive the question can be. I also caution you against using this approach with others – as it can be somewhat annoying.

ACTIVITY   What would that mean for me?

Think of something that you want, but that you don't yet have. To each answer, repeatedly ask yourself the question 'And what would that mean for me?'

For example:

If I got that promotion *what would that mean for me?*

More money

... and what would that mean for me?

More things

... and what would that mean for me?

More enjoyment in life

... and what would that mean for me?

More happiness...

What can you do?

Whatever your genetic make-up, you can choose to focus on the positive in any situations. In Chapter 5 I described the research finding that the negative has a bigger impact than the positive (the cockroach in the bowl of cherries).

It's the same at work. Sure, there will be the 'event' that takes your attention – 'you can't believe what she did/said' – but you may want to think about how you provide your mind with a good balance which seems to account for higher levels of well-being.

I'm not suggesting it's easy to 'force' yourself to refocus your attention. It takes practice. For many of us, dedicated, regular, repeated practice does not come naturally. It's the art of self-discipline.

If it's that hard, why would I want to do it?

Whilst self-discipline is not always easy, when it comes to your happiness, it's worth it. For many of us happiness is the value (thing that's important) which underpins many of our 'wants' in life. Whilst you may still want the promotion, in practice, authentic happiness brings you more happiness in the long term. Of course, having both may be your ideal. As you stay focused on the desired outcome of promotion, along with practising the skills of working with others, effective team collaboration, being open to new opportunities ... you will start to differentiate your skills, attitudes and habits from others.

One element of self-mastery is looking after our physical body, which includes paying attention to nutrition, sleep and physical activity. These things may not be at the forefront of our mind when preparing for great days at work, but they are important. Some people care more for their cars more than they do their body, and whilst car safety is important, it should not be at the expense of your corporal well-being.

However well we're genetically wired for happiness there is the opportunity to modify up to 60 per cent of our wiring. 'Happiness' may seem a 'fluffy' inconsequential life pursuit, but it does underpin many of our aspirations. Of course, however well we set our vision, focus on our emotional well-being and strive to achieve goals, there are likely to be some setbacks. It's not the obstacles, but how we deal with them. The following section provides you with some useful tools for dealing with life's challenges.

Dealing with obstacles

Experience is not what happens to a man; it is what a man does with what happens to him.
Aldous Huxley

Just when the caterpillar thought the world was over, it became a butterfly.
Anonymous

This section is about gaining a better understanding of how we can deal with the inevitable obstacles and challenges that life presents us with.

The first aspect we'll explore is identifying your natural strengths. One way to think of your strengths is like a utility belt with a set of tools that you have 'out of the box'. The combination of tools and the way in which you choose to use them is pretty unique to you. A useful first step is to identify these tools, ie to become familiar with your natural strengths. You can of course add tools and skills to your kit bag.

Following a discussion on strengths, we'll take a look at how you can expand your coping skills so that you can quickly bounce back from set backs and disappointments, because another key feature of successful people is how they bounce back and have resilience.

Character strengths

Knowing your strengths gives you a strong foundation on which to grow.

British humour tends to encourage the ability to laugh at ourselves. Often however, our humour can be self-deprecating, which combined with our past negative storytelling tendencies can have an overall negative impact. This focus on the negative can mean that we unwittingly undermine some of our core strengths.

> My ability to navigate has improved greatly with the use of 'sat nav lady'. However, were I to focus on my ability to get lost, and use negative self-talk, not only would I undermine myself, I would increase my stress every time I wanted to go somewhere without the help of GPS.

We often overlook what comes easily to us. Typically within a work culture the focus is on addressing weaknesses, and often people develop considerable skills in their weaker areas. By contrast, strengths are a great way to think about activities in your life that you're good at *and* that you enjoy, and therefore are intrinsically motivating. These can be the activities that you naturally seek out.

So just what are your strengths? You may already know some of them, which is great. If you don't, then taking a 'personal inventory' is a good starting point. Over the page are a number of different approaches although to get an inventory you may only want to do one or two.

How do you find your strengths?

There are different ways you can find out about your strengths:

- Reflect; make a list; you know some of them already.
- You can ask others – either formally or informally.
- Realise 2 provide a relatively inexpensive standard questionnaire at: **http://www.cappeu.com/Realise2.aspx**.
- Strengths finder is based on research by Gallup at: **http://www.strengthsfinder.com**.
- Additionally, there are several psychometric tools that can provide you with insights about your natural style, which in turn provide insights into your strengths. For example, the Myers–Briggs Type Indicator (MBTI) is a useful starting point, as is DISC.

I have used MBTI with well over 1,500 people. It's a great way for people not only to discover their strengths, but to realize that other people have different strengths. This can enhance communication and increases impact and influence. You may find that you have some 'aha!' moments as you understand why you or someone else behaves in the way they do.

Whichever approach you use, the key point is to discover your particular strengths, in order to maximize your use of them. That doesn't mean use them to the exclusion of everything else – but it might mean that you could explore other areas in your life in which you could also use them.

It can be useful to remember that others may enjoy the jobs you don't. Whilst there are probably tasks that no one relishes you may want to simply ask colleagues some questions to see if there are some happy swaps to be done. Here are a couple of examples:

At the beginning of my corporate career when I was in an IT support role, I realized that there were some things I was more suited to than others. At one point I had to write a short computer program in a language called REXX – not something I enjoyed or had a natural aptitude for. My colleague Luke was responsible for meeting a client – not a task he relished (whereas he loved programming). You can tell where this is going. For that day we swapped tasks. He wrote the program code for me – and I undertook his client meeting. I always managed to swap the programming that I had to do. The downside is that I never developed my programming skills.

The downside of strengths

The implication is that strengths are fixed, and a person only grows by finding new ways to use existing strengths. However, this doesn't give people the sense that they can develop new strengths. Therefore there's a slight risk that strengths 'overdone' or used to an extreme encourages a fixed mindset. For example: 'This is what I'm good at, either give me some of that or leave me alone.' This can be seen in my example of trying not to program. My mindset was more fixed around the skill of programming. However, new skills can be learned and become strengths.

One high-profile example of learning new skills is Formula 1 racing driver Alex Zanardi, who having been involved in a racing accident had both his legs amputated. Although he returned to motor sport, he also started competing in handbiking. At the London 2012 Paralympics he won gold medals in several categories of handbiking.

In Zanardi's case, he probably has a strength around 'competitiveness'. He found another area of life in which to use it. However, strengths should enable rather than limit you. Strengths may be a good starting point, especially if you've never done this type of activity before. They point to healthy behaviours, something positive to focus on and talk to others about. However, strengths are just a device, and more important is the flexibility to adapt one's behaviour to the 'here and now' reality (Kashdan and Rottenberg, 2010).

For many people strength tools offer simple yet powerful insights. Without ignoring the value from strengths, also remember that it's just one way of seeing the world. Take what you can from the tools – they should enable rather than limit you.

Sometimes life events can challenge and shake our worldview. How come after some significant events some people seem to come out the other side thriving, whereas others continue to be morose? One of the skills – which can be learned – is our ability to 'bounce back'.

Bounce back

You must never confuse faith that you will prevail in the end – which you can never afford to lose – with the discipline to confront the most brutal facts of your current reality, whatever they might be.

James Stockdale (2001)

The above quote is from James Stockdale, who ran for US vice president in 1992. Prior to that he had been the highest-ranking naval officer held as a Vietnamese prisoner of war. He was repeatedly tortured, held in solitary confinement and not given any reason to believe that he would be released.

Stockdale later commented: 'I never lost faith in the end of the story, I never doubted not only that I would get out, but also that I would prevail in the end and turn the experience into the defining event of my life, which, in retrospect, I would not trade.' You may notice what seems to be an element of benefit finding (described in Chapter 5.) Benefit finding is the ability to look back at an experience, however ghastly it seemed at the time, and distil the benefits.

I think Stockdale's example demonstrates the ability to bounce back and thrive despite harsh reality. While I expect for the majority of us being captured in warfare is not part of the day-to-day risks we face within our normal work day, there is a lot to learn from people who have experienced trauma, and bounced back.

The adversities that we face in civilian life may be different, but having the skills and tools to deal with hardships and misfortunes is useful whatever our circumstances. Stress is caused when we don't have the tools to cope with the demands of the situation or environment. Each of us has a different set of tools which is why the particular circumstances which cause stressful situations are not the same for each of us.

> *Psychological stress refers to a relationship with the environment that the person appraises as significant for his or her well-being and in which the demands tax or exceed available coping resources.*
> Lazarus and Folkman (1987)

When you have great days at work it's likely that there will be sufficient challenge, but not so much challenge as to overwhelm you and lead you to experience high levels of stress. In order to experience less stress, develop your coping skills. There is a significant amount of research around the topic of resilience, which is the ability of a person to 'come through' a significant event well.

In my career there was one job that I remember being turned down for and being disappointed. I knew I had a choice in how I responded: would I turn away from what I had hoped would be my dream job? Would the rejection make me more determined and work even harder to get the job? Yes, you guessed it, I worked harder and got the job about a year later. In hindsight I think I was more determined to succeed at the job, and I gained valuable experience in the interim.

Research by Cecilia Cheng (2003) suggests that there are four areas that many of us can develop in order to be more effective at dealing with the unexpected:

1 Broaden our coping skills repertoire.

2 Be able to generate more strategies to deal with the stressful situation.

3 Enhance our understanding of when to use these strategies effectively.

4 Reduce the need for closure.

These are discussed further below.

Broaden our coping skills repertoire

There are many ways people react in difficult situations. One group of researchers found over 400 different ways that people cope with stress. Broadly speaking there are three main responses to stress, from the simple, but not effective approach of avoiding problems, to the more active approaches of problem- or task-focused and emotion-focused coping strategies.

Avoidance, or distraction, activities often take the form of taking one's mind off the situation – but without the intention of doing that. The range of distraction activities is huge, but might involve sleeping more than usual, shopping or calling a friend, but for distraction rather than for assistance either in the task or for emotional support.

Task-focused, or problem-focused, coping is more active, and includes planning and asking for assistance. It is useful when the stressful events are controllable, but can lead to increased stress when events are outside of your control:

- This is more situationally dependent, but it can be useful to take a moment to think about your successes in this area so that you can repeat them.
- In past situations that you successfully planned, what did you learn?
- Who could you call for assistance?

Emotion-focused coping includes seeking social support for emotional reasons, positive reinterpretation of events, acceptance and humour. Emotion-focused coping strategies have a stress-relieving role in events which are uncontrollable, but this approach is not so useful when you can take control of the event:

- Who can you call for support?
- What activities can you do to let off steam?
- What activities do you find calming?
- Where do you get your inspiration?
- What music relaxes you?
- Which film or comedy never ceases to have you in fits of laughter?
- What type of calming breathing works for you?

It's not surprising to learn that we experience less stress if we use the appropriate coping strategy for the situation. And each of us can use both emotion- and task-focused coping approaches. The wiring is certainly in place, although you may not have experience with one or other technique. Within each category there is a broad range of specific techniques, but it's not uncommon for people to rely on just one form of coping style.

Generate more strategies

From my personal experience I know that it's been useful for me to think ahead, thinking about other coping strategies I could use in advance of a stressful situation. I recommend that you take a couple of minutes to add to your existing repertoire.

Within business, can you occasionally display your vulnerability by asking for assistance? Even if not in your immediate work environment, can you ask your broader network? If the answer is 'never', you may wish to take another look at Chapter 2 on developing a growth mindset. This is because it may indicate a rigidity in the way you think which may suggest more of a fixed mindset.

ACTIVITY Coping strategies

What coping strategies do you typically use? What coping strategies could you add? How will you remember to use your strategy in a time of 'crisis'?

When to use which strategy effectively

Cecilia Cheng also suggests an effective way to choose which strategy to use in each situation is by asking:

> If *the outcome of the stressful situation is amenable to change,* then *use the problem-focused coping.* If *the outcome of the stressful situation is not amenable to change,* then *use emotion-focused coping.*

It sounds easy, and yet deep in the midst of overwhelm it can be harder to search and use new coping strategies; that's one of the reasons it's useful to have a plan.

Reducing the need for closure

Encountering a stressful event provokes a considerable amount of ambiguity and uncertain feelings. Cheng's research also looked at why individuals are flexible or rigid in their use of coping strategy. She's shown that people who have a higher need for closure experience more discomfort in ambiguous situations. They are also more susceptible to the adverse impact of stress than were their counterparts with a lower need for closure.

The need for closure is a motivational force that influences things including person perception and judgement. Individuals higher in need for closure are more motivated to bring information processing to a close by leaping to a conclusion.

The research suggests that when individuals can see that they have more elaborate ways to deal with a stressful situation, they show greater coping flexibility.

The final topic for this chapter is developing a sense of perspective.

A sense of perspective

Several years ago, as part of some research on the different cognitive and emotional approaches to learning, I interviewed people who were fluent in a second language. I asked participants how they dealt with making mistakes. One research participant explained she came to the UK from a war zone and described the sense of perspective this experience had given her; in her everyday life in the UK, making a few grammatical mistakes has minimal implications.

I think we can all develop a sense of perspective by asking 'Will this matter in five or ten years from now?' In a YouTube video created from Steve Jobs's speech to Stanford graduates in 2005 he talked about his 'death question'. He said that each morning he would ask himself: 'If today were the last day of my life would I want to do what I am about to do today?' He goes on to say: 'Whenever the answer has been "no" for too many days in a row, I know I need to change something.'

> *What you do today is important because you are exchanging a day of your life for it.*
>
> Anon

Being aware of our mortality can keep things in perspective and can also ensure that we're doing what we love to do. Finding and using your strengths is one way to ensure you're doing what you love.

This chapter also explored aspects of your physiology and asked if you treat your car better than you treat your body. There is much that you can do to keep your body in good order, from getting appropriate nutrition, drinking the recommended amounts of water and getting enough exercise and sleep.

For most of us, strength provides a robust platform from which to celebrate our uniqueness and grow.

The chapter then introduced and broadened your coping strategies, to give you new options in times of crisis. The time to explore these options and put a plan in place is typically not when you're in the middle of a crisis, but now, when you're feeling more upbeat.

However well you manage yourself, your situation and emotions – in the work environment there are other people. These others can either enhance our days or have the effect of bringing us down. You can't change other people, but you can change your interactions with them – which in turn may change how they respond to you. The next chapter focuses on work relationships.

Summary

- Your mind and body are linked.

- You know what to do, eat good food, little and often, and for most of us it also involves eating more fruit and veg.

- Drink sufficient quantities of water.

- Get enough sleep.

- Aim to do 30 minutes of physical activity daily.

- Know your strengths and think creatively about how else you can use them.

- Develop your skills to 'bounce back' from a crisis; most of us revert to either task-focused or emotion-focused strategies for coping – and different situations benefit from different coping approaches.

- Develop the skill of seeing situations, events and people from different perspectives. Whether it be putting yourself in someone else's shoes, the perspective of time or context.

More information

DISC: http://en.wikipedia.org/wiki/DISC_assessment

European Food Information Council: http://www.eufic.org/article/en/artid/New-nutrition-guidelines-Europe-halfway-there/

European Food Safety Authority: http://www.efsa.europa.eu/en/efsajournal/doc/1459.pdf

HeartMath: http://www.heartmath.org/free-services/tools-for-well-being/tools-for-well-being-home.html

Myers-Briggs: http://www.myersbriggs.org/my-mbti-personality-type/mbti-basics

Steve Jobs, Stanford Address: **http://tinyurl.com/ec4jo and** http://www.youtube.com/watch?v=D1R-jKKp3NA

Part Four
THE ART AND SCIENCE OF COMMUNICATIONS

10
Working
with others

No man is an island, entire of itself.

John Donne

Humans are essentially social creatures and as such, interpersonal relationships are of central importance for well-being and overall happiness and thus for experiencing great days at work. The list of benefits of having social relationships is a long one, and includes improved physical, mental and emotional quality of life, and better coping responses to stress and adversity. Having relationships is more beneficial than not having relationships and of course 'good' relationships are better than bad. Social relationships are predictors of overall satisfaction with life, reducing illness symptoms and developing meaning in life. Individuals who experience more negative moods are more likely to experience poor interpersonal relations (Froh *et al*, 2007).

Maintaining and enhancing social relationships are 'robustly related to subjective well-being and an overall enhancement in quality of life' (Froh *et al*, 2007). Whereas Lyubomirsky, (2010) describes: 'One of the strongest findings in literature on happiness is that happy people have better relationships than their less happy peers.'

It seems that having good social relationships starts an upward spiral of success and happiness. Not all relationships are the same quality (see later in this chapter), which does not suggest that you ditch low-quality relationships. But you can be discerning as to whom you spend your time with. Spend more time with people who are enthusiastic and supportive, and contribute to you having more great days at work.

Outside of work we have the ability to choose whom we spend time with. Within the workplace it is rare to get the same amount of choice of who your co-workers are and you may work with a whole range of people to complete tasks. This chapter will give you the building blocks of how to form effective working relationships. Because most relationships 'just work', usually people don't pay much attention to how they form work relationships. This chapter will look more closely at some of the components of a healthy working relationship so that you can actively go out and create more effective work relationships.

Chapters 11 and 12 take work relationships to the next level by exploring the dynamics of relationships at work in two particular contexts: creating high-performing teams and negotiations.

Although we may not believe that in work we can have the same degree of control over who we spend our time with as we do in our personal life, there is a lot we can do to influence our interactions, and increase the likelihood that the relationship generates energy rather than draining it.

A Gallup survey found that having what they described as a 'best friend at work' was important (Buckingham and Coffman, 2005). The benefits include having someone to bounce ideas off and who may see things differently from you. In times of crisis they can provide problem- or emotion-focused support. In times of joy they can provide moments of shared savouring and good company.

What do relationships give you?

There are many ways in which a social network can provide us with support. First are a few suggestions, followed by tips for how you can develop supporting relationships.

Different perspective

Sometimes the way we see the problem is the problem.

Covey

The above statement contains much truth. Because we are unique we tend to see things differently from others, so getting someone else's perspective can shed a different light on the problem.

Sometimes just the act of describing the situation can provide insight and break an ineffective thinking cycle going round and round in your head. In times of stress someone who truly has a different perspective may provide you with additional ways to 'cope', whether this is emotion- or task-based coping.

Broadening your network

Whilst formal organizational hierarchies are useful, often work gets done and information gets passed through our informal networks. This information may be pertinent to your job, or it may be about finding new opportunities in different parts of the business. And sometimes it's just nice to meet with different people. It's useful to have a network, or range of people to call upon for assistance. Perhaps someone in your network has experienced a similar situation and can provide some advice, and it's great when we return the favour and support others in their quest.

Many people only think of their network when they are facing a major change that has been foisted on them, for example redundancy, a change in boss etc. Certainly, in today's world a burst of activity or an updated profile on a networking site could be a signal of a CV being updated. However, networks are a whole lot more than the stepping stone to the next job – they are part of the informal communication connections that bind companies together, and they're the informal exchange of ideas which spark creativity. Throughout society, meeting places have been important for the transmission of information. Don't lose sight of the importance of face-to-face communication. While e-mail and Facebook have their place, as do Skype and video conferencing, where it's possible, for full spectrum communication nothing can beat face-to-face contact.

Social aspects

Perhaps the support of others encourages you, or maybe they just make you smile and laugh – and those positive emotions have the 'broaden and build' effect described in Chapter 6.

I knew a senior consultant in a large corporate who made a point of not going to lunch in the canteen on his own. At first I thought it was his insecurity, but he just found it nicer and more pleasurable to sit with enjoyable company: it's a mini-form of relaxation during the day! Other obvious benefits are that it's an opportunity to meet with people outside of your department – for different insights, you just have to do it.

Another manager said that on first becoming a manager she was so busy that she really resented going for coffee with her team because she was not able to get on with her work. As soon as she realized that going for coffee was an important part of her job (in that she got a feel of the team's morale and any concerns) she started to relax about it, and actually enjoyed it!

Developing supportive relationships

Whilst the particular reasons why having a social network is so beneficial have so far eluded scientists, there is no doubt as to their importance. What follows are techniques for developing your skills in working with, and relating to, others at work. I describe some of the building blocks of relationships and communication in the two subsequent chapters and then describe how these skills are applied both within teams and as part of negotiations.

Initiating

Ulrich and Ulrich (2010) suggest that social relations at work begin with making and receiving 'bids'. Relationship expert John Gottman defines a bid as a request for attention. This might be a smile, saying hello, offering a compliment, requesting help or asking a question:

> In the world of relationships nothing happens until someone makes a bid ... equally important in the bidding process is the response we get to our bids. If the other party does not respond by paying attention to our bid in a positive way the game stops, like a ball that dies when a tennis serve is not returned. Unlike the tennis serve, the goal of the bid is not to defeat the opponent but to encourage a volley.
>
> Ulrich and Ulrich (2010)

That is not to suggest that the volley continues indefinitely, or that you're looking to compete with the record-breaking marathon tennis match[1] at the 2010 Wimbledon Championships! Typically in the work environment our communications take place around particular tasks or settings which have a natural and finite term.

TIP

In group situations, most people wait to be introduced like a guest. You can initiate conversations. Take the initiative, act like the host, and initiate introductions and conversations.

Curiosity

One key skill in building relationships is being interested in others. In business we can sometimes be too quick to jump to conclusions, which can lead to negative consequences based on incomplete or missing information. Sometimes when others give us information, we might think 'No, you're wrong!' In those moments, before you open your mouth you may want to employ some curiosity, an open mindset, and ask a few questions. Entertain the thought that perhaps the other person might have more information than you do about the situation, therefore your job in the conversation is to discover some of the missing facts. Hopefully it's not hard to see the difference between: 'Why on earth did you do that?' and 'I'm curious, what led you to that decision?'

When the situation is emotionally charged, perhaps the former is the first question that will come to mind. However, the second question will be far more productive and encourage a higher quality of response in that you're more likely to discover what the other person is thinking rather than provoke a defensive response. Therefore, please pay attention to both the words that you use and the *tone* of your voice.

We all like to feel heard. Having curiosity about what the person's talking about is an essential ingredient in building rapport. With rapport you build trust to say 'no' later, or to question – without burning the relationship.

Questions

At some point, you may have been on a course which extols the virtues of questions. I'm a firm believer in the power of questions, and possibly slightly evangelical on the topic. Many people know the theory of questions – but are less fluent speaking the language of questions.

Here's a very quick recap on the differences between closed and open questions. A closed question is one that elicits a one-word answer and often starts 'do you ...?', 'have you ...?', 'is it ...?', where technically the answer is 'yes' or 'no'. Whilst people may respond more fully, they don't have to 'think' too hard.

By contrast, an open question demonstrates that your thinking is open – and you seek information. Open questions can be very powerful since they can direct the course of a conversation. For example, if you want to hear about the reasons why something can't be done, ask, 'What's the reason this isn't possible?' If however you're more interested in finding solutions you could ask, 'How do you think we could get round this?'

Open Questions: What, Why, How, Who, When, Where

The first three generally provide the most information. The last three could be answered in a word. The 'why' question normally has a caution around its use as it can invoke defensiveness – 'Why did you do it that way?' – because for some people there is an implied criticism.

TIP

Ask more open questions: 'What do you think about that?'

TIP

Listen to the response! Nod to show that you've heard. If you need time to consider your response – just say: 'What you've said is thought provoking, I'm thinking of the best way to respond.'

Effective responding

'I've got some good news!' How do you respond when colleagues or friends share their good news with you?

There are a variety of ways you could react:

- You could be happy for them, but not make a big deal about it.
- You could be indifferent ('Oh').
- You could be sceptical, and point out why the good news isn't so good at all ('Are you sure that this is what you really want? Isn't it a bit risky?').

Researchers (Gable *et al*, 2004) found there's a really effective way to respond. It's called 'active constructive' and essentially means that you react in an active-constructive way by:

- feeling genuine excitement;
- outwardly displaying your excitement;
- capitalizing (prolonging discussion of the good news, telling people about it, suggesting celebratory activities).

Figure 10.1 gives some examples.

FIGURE 10.1   Active constructive responding

Passive and constructive	Active and constructive
'That's good news.'	'That's great, I know how important that promotion was to you! We should go out and celebrate and you can tell me what excites you most about your new job.'
(Non-verbal communication: little or no active emotional expression)	(Non-verbal communication: maintaining good eye contact; displays of positive emotions such as genuine smiling, laughter and appropriate touch)
Passive and destructive	**Active and destructive**
'What are we doing on Friday night?'	'That sounds like a lot of responsibility to take on. There will probably be more stress involved in the new position and longer hours at the office.'
(Non-verbal communication: little or no eye contact, turning away, leaving the room)	(Non-verbal communication: displays of negative emotions such as furrowed brow, frowning)

Adapted from Gable *et al* (2004) and Hefferon workshop presentation (2011)

'Active and constructive' is the top-right box. Before you think it's a bit too 'gushy', try to stand in the other person's shoes, or imagine a time when someone – probably close to you – was happy and enthusiastic for you. In my experience people love to be on the receiving end of it – so try it out and watch the response you get.

Those of you who might describe yourself as a strong silent type may prefer the passive and constructive – however, whilst it seems supportive, it doesn't have the same positive impact on the other person. The research clearly shows that these comments are not sufficient to develop the relationship. In the next chapter we see that it's comments like these that form the basis of high-performing teams where everyone is riding high at the top of their game.

TIP

Respond to other people's good news with an outward display of genuine enthusiasm and ask for more information: 'That's sounds like great news, how did that come about?'

You may think that active constructive is a bit gushy, but watch the response when you use it genuinely!

There are people in your life for whom you're delighted to share in their good news – and there doesn't have to be anything in it for you! More importantly there may be people you don't care for but you can genuinely share (albeit only for a couple of minutes) their good news in an 'active-constructive' manner: you have the potential to significantly shift the relationship forward. Do not be put off by any initial scepticism especially if this is the first positive interaction you have had together.

Assertive communications

Not all relationships are healthy (some are draining and unproductive), so how do you form healthy relationships? This section will explore what it means to be assertive at work – a key skill in forming healthy relationships – and then we will look at some dynamics of relationships, suggesting ways of steering your relationships more towards health.

Sadly I think sometimes the word 'assertive' has become a byword for 'aggressive behaviour' and 'bully'. In order to ensure we are aligned on what the terms mean, let's first take a look at some definitions. In their book *Assertiveness at Work* (1999), Ken and Kate Back describe:

- Aggressiveness: behaving as if my needs, rights and wants are more important than yours.
- Non-assertive: behaving as if my needs, rights and wants are less important than yours.
- Assertiveness: behaving as if my needs, rights and wants are equal to yours.

Whilst in the short term aggressive behaviour might get fast results, over time people who have been bullied are likely to get cheesed off and not produce results, withdraw or deliberately become obstructive or unproductive. Being non-assertive can leave people feeling resentful that others haven't noticed them. In my experience the key skill is to use assertive communication. This ensures that focus remains on the job to be done. Too much 'pandering' happens in organizations, whether others are pandering to our whims or we to theirs. In the meantime very little productive work is happening as a result of all that pandering!

Even in a hierarchical organization as an individual you have 'equal needs, rights and wants' both to those senior to you, and those more junior to you. This means you have a right to your opinion, they have a right to theirs. These opinions may be different. Whilst opinions are cheap – everyone has them – in a business setting, information has currency. The information that each of you has will be different. You may have information based on the detail of the project or task you're working on, whereas your manager may have a broader perspective. Both sets of information will be useful. Remember many minds and perspectives focused on finding solutions will be more effective than just one.

When there is a difference of opinion don't just railroad the other person or back down. I often hear that in situations where opinions differ, people compromise. For me that has negative connotations.

COMPROMISE

You may have heard the story of two cooks, each requiring a lemon for their recipe, but with only one available. Their compromise is to have half a lemon each ... which is OK until you realize that one cook required the zest, and the other the juice. 'If only' they had found out a little more about the specific requirements of the situation then they each could have had exactly what they needed.

Compromise seems to be an easy option when the focus is on keeping one another happy, rather than the art and skills of asking questions in an assertive manner, and finding facts. Of course there are different decision-making strategies, the satisficer and the maximizer, covered more fully in Chapter 8 – and it's also about deciding the impact of the decision and which strategy is good enough!

It's often useful to 'negotiate' a solution based on what's required.

Mixed messages from academic research

In the academic literature assertiveness relates to the concept of self-esteem. The science of self-esteem is fragmented with mixed implications. Back in the 1970s self-esteem was seen to be a significant factor in determining academic success in school-aged children. Unfortunately research also links high self-esteem to bullying. 'The highest and lowest rates of cheating and bullying are found in different sub-categories of high self-esteem' (Baumeister *et al*, 2003). So in building self-esteem or assertiveness, there is a risk of becoming a bully.

The discrepancy between views can be explained because the scientific measurement of self-esteem is determined without reference to other people. If a person has high self-esteem, but holds others in low regard, it's likely that bullying will take place. If, however, a person has high self-esteem and also holds other people in equally high regard then bullying is not likely.

Based on the definitions of assertiveness and aggressiveness mentioned above, then it seems bullies have been perhaps unwittingly encouraged to put themselves first, disregarding others. In the workplace, most 'bullies' don't see themselves as bullies.

Building assertiveness

Rather than building self-esteem and assertive behaviours in isolation from others, I think it's useful to think about them in relation to other people. What follows is an approach which helps to ensure communications remain assertive without developing self-esteem which verges on bullying behaviours. In corporate training and executive one to one work with clients, the tool I often use for understanding the dynamics in relationships is the OK Corral. The specifics of this tool have been adapted from work by Momentum Consultants, who in turn adapted them from the field of Transactional Analysis (TA). TA is a theory of personality and a psychotherapy for personal growth and personal change. Because of the importance of having healthy relationships with others in order to lead to having more great days at work, we will take a closer look at this powerful tool.

The OK Corral

The OK Corral is the name of a model developed by Franklin Ernst which maps how a person views *themselves* and *others* in terms of 'OKness'.

Ernst (1971) plotted the statements on a grid[2] (see Figure 10.2), with the 'I'm OK' to 'I'm not OK' on the vertical continuum, and 'You're OK' to 'You're not OK' on the horizontal continuum. In describing the OK Corral Stewart and Joines (1987) noted that by putting these together in all their possible combinations, the following four statements about self and others emerge:

FIGURE 10.2   OK Corral – adaptation

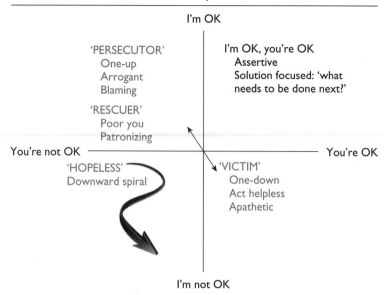

I'm OK

'PERSECUTOR'
One-up
Arrogant
Blaming

I'm OK, you're OK
Assertive
Solution focused: 'what
needs to be done next?'

'RESCUER'
Poor you
Patronizing

You're not OK   You're OK

'HOPELESS'
Downward spiral

'VICTIM'
One-down
Act helpless
Apathetic

I'm not OK

Adapted from Ernst (1971), Karpman (1968) and Momentum Consultants

- I'm OK, you're OK.
- I'm not OK, you're OK.
- I'm OK, you're not OK.
- I'm not OK, you're not OK.

The diagram provides a way of understanding the reinforcing automatic dynamics that sometimes happen between people, which I believe can lead to less healthy relationships.

The key insight or benefit of the OK Corral is to recognize that however (badly) another person communicates with you, you don't have to respond automatically, as though you're a puppet with the other person pulling your strings. You have choice. The trick, of course, is to be able to catch yourself before you react and, as with all new skills, it might require a bit of practice!

The focus of this book is on healthy relationships, and specifically ones that lead to having great days at work. Therefore, I'll briefly describe some of the behaviours typical in each of the

FIGURE 10.3   Responding to others like a puppet on a string

quadrants before exploring how you can use this to develop your relationships.

Whilst we might habitually communicate from only one of the four quadrants, we can and do communicate from all of them. This is entirely normal. What follows is how you can become increasingly aware of the underlying dynamic of a conversation so that you don't have to respond with a knee-jerk reaction, but can have a more considered response, thus developing your gravitas in any situation.

Overview of behaviours in each quadrant

Conceptually understanding the OK Corral doesn't take long – the value, and the challenge is in developing awareness and on-going practice in using it. Therefore, when you have had one of 'those' conversations, you know, the one where you wonder just *how* and *why* you agreed to do something or where you 'snapped' in an 'out of character way' – or indeed any conversation where you think

'What happened there?' – it's probably a good cue to come back and look at this tool to try and understand what happened.

In order to start developing awareness, tune in to your responses. You probably recognize the type of things that people you know say in each of the quadrants: imagine someone saying the initial sentences to you. There is no right or wrong way to respond, but experience the emotional impact, and what you'd like to do or say in response. You may not be able to 'name' the emotional impact, in which case just note your instinctive response. It's likely that one or more of the phrases will cause you to have a particular reaction – that's great, make a note. Then we will look at why they might have that effect and some of the antidotes.

You're OK, I'm not OK ('victim')

(For emphasis, imagine this being said a slight whine.) 'Gosh, that's hard, I'm not sure that I can do it. It's OK for you, you've got lots of experience – I'll never be any good at it.'

Behaviour in this quadrant typically operates from being 'one-down', slightly helpless.

Notice, what's the emotional impact on you? How do you want to respond?

You're not OK, I'm OK ('persecutor' behaviour)

(For added arrogance, imagine it being said by someone who is rolling their eyes as they say it. Add emphasis to the word 'bother'.) 'Am I the only one to do any work around here! I don't know why I bother trying to explain anything to you – you never do anything.' Left unsaid, but implied is the question 'Am I the only competent person around here?' or 'You're too stupid to understand this.'

Notice, what's the emotional impact on you? What's your instinctive response?

You're not OK, I'm OK ('rescuer' behaviour)

There's another manifestation of the behaviours in this quadrant.

(To increase the impact, imagine it being said in a very slow, laboured tone of voice, and add a mild patronizing tone.) 'This piece of work is quite complicated, but I'll describe what you need to do slowly, and I operate an open door policy for you to ask me questions at any time ...' unsaid 'You poor thing ... you need my continuing help to cope around here – good job I'm here to help.'

Notice, what's the emotional impact on you? What would you say or do in that situation?

You're not OK, I'm not OK

This can be a downward spiral of negativity. 'I can't fix the situation, and neither can you. Woe is me!'

(Imagine the person with a slouch, looking down, shaking their head.) 'The management aren't up to it, whatever I do won't make a difference – this place is doomed.'

Notice, what's the emotional impact on you? How do you want to respond?

Relationship dynamics

Before completing the quadrants and describing I'm OK, you're OK, you may have noticed that some of the phrases caused a more intense emotional response from you than others, which is very normal.

In the work environment there can be relationship dynamics between 'victims' and 'persecutors' or 'rescuers' – each 'needing' each other to reinforce their view of the world.

An example which demonstrates a negative relationship and negative effect on self-esteem is when a person displays 'victim' behaviour in a given situation, and is likely to feel 'one-down' to another person. They may have an unconscious expectation for people to behave in a certain way, either by rescuing or persecuting, which reinforces their 'one-down' view of the world, which in turn reinforces their negative self-esteem. So what's the alternative?

Essentially we return to the definition of assertiveness – where we have needs, rights and wants which are held to be equal. Sometimes easier said than done, but by being aware of what is going on we can start taking action which will immediately start to empower us. Assertiveness, gravitas and long term credibility are in the realm of the I'm OK, you're OK quadrant.

I'm OK, you're OK

Finally the sweet spot! I'm OK, you're OK is effective in problem-solving, assertive situations. That is not to say there is anything wrong with the others – they are all a natural part of human behaviour. It's just that I'm OK, you're OK maintains relations for the long run. Each situation is different, but the key is not to be hooked by your instinctive response.

Responding to the 'victim': it's natural to either want to 'help' or to verbally 'slap'. However, you can engage the person and not be drawn into the emotion. You could repeat the question or ask how they could start on the task.

Responding to the 'persecutor': instinctive responses range from wanting to get into a verbal fight, or backing down sheepishly. It's useful to notice if the person uses this behaviour with other people – as typically they do. As you realize that they're not responding to you, it's just a habit that's formed in the way they respond, you could reflect back to them that they seem annoyed, and can repeat the original request.

Responding to the I'm not OK, you're not OK: this is more challenging – but the good news is that in the work environment there are fewer of these people who use this response habitually.

At work we have a number of relationships; I'm guessing that for most of us it's important for us to ensure the quality of the relationships for the long term. For example, with your colleagues you provide support or share information with each other, day in and day out. Relationships with supervisors, or even those with subordinates, are likely to be important in the long term.

The option is still available to respond to any of the quadrants instinctively. They can be used to manipulate. As a buyer I was on the receiving end of a sales person trying to bully me into the sale by suggesting that I didn't have the sign-off authority on a large sum of money. I assume he expected me to 'prove' myself by buying, but I didn't like the way he made me feel, and given there were other service providers with very similar offerings, I took the business elsewhere.

You may not hold a grudge against poor behaviour or not think twice about manipulation in the game of business – other people might. And of course there are relationships with customers and suppliers. I'm not sure that anyone likes to be backed into a corner, so I'm OK, you're OK gives a basis for negotiating without emotional blackmail.

> *People may not remember exactly what you did, or what you said, but they will always remember how you made them feel.*
>
> Maya Angelou

Knowing your strengths, developing your vision and having goals that you regularly achieve will keep you motivated.

Developing options to respond

So now you know what is going on within the dynamics of communications, next we'll look briefly at why the phrases have a 'pull', and what you can do differently in each of the situations. Each type of communication 'invites' particular responses. For example, an adult being childish may invite a parental response (which could range from being 'told off' to being nurtured). Alternatively the childish response may also invite someone to join in with their playfulness. Sometimes the response we get from others can be telling about the signals we're putting into the world. One way to determine how effective our communication is the response we get.

TIP

If you feel someone's comment is having an emotional impact on you (from any of the quadrants): Breathe. Reflect back what they've said. Ask a question.

You're OK, I'm not OK ('victim' behaviours)

The implied invitation is for you to respond from 'rescuer': 'OK, I'll help you with that ... ' However, for some people this invitation will invoke their 'persecutor': 'For goodness sake, just get on with it!'

Remember you are not a puppet: just because the strings are pulled you still have a choice of different ways to respond. You don't have to accept the invitation to respond in this predictable way.

Antidote: stay focused on the original request, ask questions – from an I'm OK, you're OK perspective. Additionally, if appropriate, remind them of the experience that they've got that's relevant. Or ask them the steps that they can take with the experience that they've got.

I'm often asked: 'Aren't there occasions when a person genuinely needs assistance?' Yes, of course. And be aware that you don't create a dependency because you enjoy the ability to 'help others'. If you notice a significant amount of your time is spent on 'helping others', even if it's a recognized part of your role, check that you're asking the other person questions to develop their thinking and their skills.

You're not OK, I'm OK ('persecutor' behaviours)

The unsaid invitation is for you to bow to the superior knowledge and expertise of the expert. However, you might remember from Chapter 2 on mindsets that when someone is so convinced of their superior knowledge, they may be suffering from an acute episode of a fixed mindset!

Antidote: say '*I'm OK, you're OK*'. Take a breath, it's generally better to stay in control of your emotions, whether their invitation provokes you to want to join them in jousting with superiority, or whether you want to withdraw from the conversation. If you're asking for information you can repeat the request. Ideally keep the behaviour separate from the person. They may be behaving in a frustrated or antagonistic way, but that is not their identity.

It's useful to remember that a person is more than their behaviour. I think it can be a little risky to stereotype an individual based on their behaviour; I've made mistakes and had momentary lapses in behaviour; I wouldn't like to be categorized hereafter based on those mistakes, would you?

> 'Two spelling mistakes and an incorrect use of the word "their"' was the feedback I received from a senior manager when submitting a report that I'd extensively researched and written. These initial comments in a conversation left me devastated. As I had a tendency to catastrophize, I thought my career was over – 'How careless, he won't trust me with anything now.' Over time I've managed to separate my mistakes and behaviour from my identity so that it doesn't overwhelm me.

I'm asked, 'What if I have made a genuine mistake and the other person has a genuine reason to be annoyed?' Then I would advocate the use of an apology. 'What if the person has the reputation of flying off the handle – nothing I'm going to do will make any difference.' Well that's great: it sounds like flying off the handle is this person's habit – and whatever you do is not likely to make a difference.

When you experience someone who habitually flies off the handle, you could consider this your 'extreme' practice of saying 'I'm OK, you're OK'.

Interestingly a significant number of people like to test models to the extreme. When discussing the separation of identity and behaviour I'm regularly asked how that applies to working with murderers. I believe that the tool still works, and I suggest that those working in a therapeutic setting with these individuals have undertaken advanced training in the area.

Fortunately, the corridors of our offices are not filled with murderers, but with genuinely nice people: essentially people just like you and me. Sometimes we all have 'off days', and sometimes people get set in patterns of behaviour that were once successful, but over time have become fossilized and rigid. If it is possible, look through the behaviour and see the person. It will make interacting with them easier and less stressful for you.

You're not OK, I'm OK ('rescuer' behaviour)

The unspoken invitation is for you to be grateful to the superior knowledge and expertise of the expert. Although for many it can provoke a bit of persecutor behaviour in response. The rescuer then switches to victim behaviour, with a mournful 'I was only trying to help' – the 'excitement' of the switch can be the foundation of many office dramas: 'He said ... then she said ..., then you'll never guess what happened next ... '. Not very productive behaviour in the workplace, and better left to TV drama.

Antidote: stay focused on the original request, ask questions – from an I'm OK, you're OK perspective.

You're not OK, I'm not OK

In the workplace setting, this set of behaviours is relatively rare on an on-going basis. Often people who experience these behaviours on a regular basis are not in employment. However, as with all of the styles of behaving we can all slip into each of them. Rath (Rath and Clifton, 2005) describes people who sap your energy, and advocates staying away from 'dippers'.

Developing OKness

In my experience of working and training others in the OK Corral, the first step is for people to notice that their internal responses are connected to the behaviours displayed by others. They then understand how to do something different, which seems to empower – I trust the same will be true for you too.

Then there's just the small matter of practising a set of skills: awareness of what's going on in the moment (Chapter 5), pausing and choosing how to respond most effectively.

The OK Corral suggests that there are two ways to develop our self-esteem: firstly through ourselves and secondly in our relationships with others, which are developed one response at a time. The previous section explored some of these responses.

We can increase our own 'OKness' with awareness of our actions, we can increase our competence in activities (practice) through which our confidence is likely to increase. The science describes this as 'mastery'. A great starting point is to know what you do well; you can develop this through understanding your strengths, and often finding ways to use more of them. Often using our strengths leads us to feeling good about ourselves.

Be supportive and encouraging of your own behaviour, which may not always be as good as you would like, but the goal is to focus and build on the positive. In Chapter 2 I talked about making mistakes as a part of developing an open mindset. This can be useful for two reasons. Firstly our own sense of self-esteem will develop if we can separate our own behaviours from our identity: 'Just because I made a spelling mistake doesn't make me a bad person.' Also, if we can perform this separation of behaviour and identity for our selves, then it's likely that we can start to practise it in relation to others. For example, 'Just because he shouted doesn't mean that he's an idiot.'

This chapter has been about illustrating the concepts of building effective relationships sufficiently to understand them. The next chapter takes further the concepts of questions, curiosity and active constructing, specifically looking at what makes a high-performing team. Then Chapter 12 further explores the skills required in negotiations.

Summary

- Many of us have never been taught how to work effectively with others – but there are some approaches that can maximize your effectiveness when working with other people.
- Responding in an 'active-constructing' way develops relationships.
- You don't have to respond instinctively to other people – you are more than a puppet being pulled by its strings.
- You can develop your skills of questioning, listening and supporting others, as well as responding to the request rather than the emotion.

Notes

1 The Isner–Mahut match which lasted for 11 hours, 5 minutes over three days.

2 The diagram has been adapted from the original and also includes behaviour labels from the Drama Triangle: Karpman, S (1968) Fairy tales and script drama analysis, *Transactional Analysis Bulletin*, 7, 39–43.

11

High-performing teams

How teams operate varies hugely. Working in a team can be a source of camaraderie, joy and productivity or just plain irritating. Often we have little choice about whether or not we work in a team, so the question is what sort of experience do you want working in a team to be? A source of on-going frustration, or a significant contributory factor in having great days at work? This chapter will explore what you can do to increase the likelihood of working in a team that is a source of energy and a contributory factor in having great days at work.

You may have a personal preference for working alone, but teamwork is becoming more prevalent so it's useful to be aware of the particular skills needed to be effective in a team, and to be able to influence the team to become high-performing. I assert that being part of a high-performing team will lead to great days at work. I'll return to the research on what makes a high-performing team, and you can decide whether you'd prefer to be part of that sub-culture or whether you'd prefer teamwork that is mediocre or less.

While working in teams is becoming more common not all people working together are a team. Sometimes it's just a 'group of people' sitting or working together, perhaps co-located, or working on the same type of thing (for example a group of solicitors or accountants who may share the same office, but would be working for different clients). Such a group of people, who are co-located but do not necessarily have shared work goals, can be thought of as a cohort. Another example is in software service divisions where there are a group of individual technical specialists who are a community or cohort but all working with separate clients. Such a group of consultants might only come together for training or 'Christmas lunch', so they are effectively separate even though they have the same employer paying their salaries. However, where there is a clearly defined common goal that everyone is working towards, then it's more than likely this group is indeed a team.

Teams often work towards meeting a challenge. All people in the team are key to the team's success, which means there is little or no internal competition. The competition comes from outside the group and can provide the stimulus for innovation, as well as drawing the group closer together.

Before looking at the research around what makes a team 'high-performing', here are a few observations on the increasing prevalence of teamwork. Increasingly, simple processes are being automated by technology, and many 'back office' functions are being sent off-shore to lower cost-base economies. You've probably been on the receiving end of a call centre based in India or the Philippines. With 'simple' tasks going abroad, what remains in the 'local' organization is becoming more complex.

In this complex environment, with increasing information available it's often unlikely that one individual has all the knowledge to solve problems alone; hence teams made up of members from different disciplines to analyse and solve problems.

However, just bringing people together doesn't mean that they will work effectively together in a team. Often training on how to work as a team is lacking. Employers assume teamwork is intuitive and everyone knows how to work as a team, but that's often not the case. People are thrown together and expected to make teamwork work. The idea behind working in teams is one of synergy: the output of two or more individuals working together will be greater than two or more individuals working separately.

Some teams are highly productive, and others are hardly effective at all. Let's look at some of the factors which influence the effectiveness of a team. Firstly, groups of people put together take a little time to form a team, and to form an effective team.

Stages of a team

These seem to be natural stages that teams go through on their way to become a 'performing' team (see Figure 11.1).

Tuckman (1965) describes the 'forming, storming, norming' stages.

The **forming** stage is characterized by politeness. Think of a parody of cocktail party introductions. Everyone's working out who's who, and what the objectives of the team are. As the initial optimism begins to fade and the reality of the task kicks in, and people vie for position, there can be some storming within the team. **Storming** is typified with a bit of 'one-upmanship', colleagues testing boundaries to see who backs down and who pushes back, over the direction of the group, the tasks and who takes ownership for what. It is a natural stage to evolve through before the team begins to find their rhythm and '**norm**', before transitioning again to the '**performing**' and high-performing team.

It is possible for a team to become stuck at any of the stages other than performing. Any change within the team (for example a new member of the team, or change of goal) will cause the team to revert to an earlier (forming) stage, albeit for a short period of time, before changing direction and moving forward again through the stages.

Teamwork doesn't come naturally to many people, and there is an assumption that we all know how to do teamwork. Often there's

FIGURE 11.1 Tuckman's stages of team development

Stage	Forming	Storming	Norming	Performing	Transforming
Characteristics	Feeling eager High expectations Some anxiety Focus on self Dependent on authority Need to establish oneself	Discrepancy between hope and reality Confusion Competition for power or authority Focus on self Frustration Conflict	Resolving discrepancies Generating agreed ways of working Developing competence Focus on team Shared responsibility	Performing at high levels Working collaboratively Self-aware Self-critical Focus on team Focus on the group winning as a whole Cooperation Excitement	Parting Celebration Closure Looking forward to next task/job
Role of the leader	Define group goals and structure Find out team members' skills and motivation Get everyone involved	Defuse conflict Channel energy/people to relevant areas Motivate and encourage Get 'buy-in' to ideas	Communicate Coach Encourage Provide resources Help people grow (through experiment and review)	Be accessible but not interfering Provide guidance if required Give feedback Stand back	Acknowledge team's achievements Review overall performance Celebrate Reward Point to the future

Adapted from Tuckman (1965)

not much training about the skills of working in a team. The next section addresses this gap so that you will know what it takes to create a dynamic team and can influence your co-workers to become a high-performing team. Achieving results, being part of a thriving group, will contribute to you having great days at work.

A fixed mindset can hold people back in teams. Some people don't like to lose face, and they perceive that questions undermine their knowledge. Not surprisingly, when questioned, they feel their idea is being attacked or challenged. In these situations, for many people it's more difficult to remain calm, and more typical to be defensive (or counter-attack). Not surprisingly, this can make working in a team not only a less pleasant experience, but also a less productive one.

As recently as a few years ago, in some organizations working in teams was potentially seen as some form of antagonistic 'debating society' where the logic of the argument and the skill and force of the narrator would 'win' others round to 'their way' of thinking. Fortunately this attitude is becoming much less prevalent. In business there is typically no single 'right' answer, therefore the growth mindset enables individuals to be open to build on their ideas, with contributions and suggestions from others, creating a synthesis of ideas – in the same way that advances in science happen (Law, 2007).

The research behind high-performing teams shows that team members typically work in a more supportive and encouraging way, and we shall take a closer look at what that means next.[1]

What does the research say?

Fredrickson and Losada (2005) analysed 60 teams and tracked every utterance of speech on four aspects:

I **Positive** or **negative** language. Language was considered *positive* if the speaker showed support, encouragement or appreciation. It was considered *negative* if the speaker demonstrated disapproval, sarcasm or cynicism.

2 **Inquiry** or **advocacy** (ask or tell). They were coded as *inquiry* if they asked questions or explored a position; they were coded as *advocacy* if they offered arguments in favour of the speaker's viewpoint or defended their own viewpoint.

3 **Self or other.** They were coded as *self* if the speaker referred to themselves, the group present or to the company itself; they were coded as *other* if the speaker referenced people or groups not present, not part of the company.

4 **Connectivity.** How attuned or responsive the teams were to one another.

Unsurprisingly, not all of the 60 teams showed high performance. The measures of performance were against three criteria: profitability, customer satisfaction and evaluation by superiors, peers and subordinates. The maths enabled cause and effect to be separated – that is, the teams were not just positive because of business results.

The findings showed that high-performance teams had unusually high positivity ratios, at about 6:1. That is, they made six positive comments to every negative comment. By contrast, low-performance teams had ratios well below 1:1 with mixed-performance teams just above this, at 2:1.

Higher-performance teams also had higher connectivity, asked questions as much as they defended their own views, and cast their attention outward as much as inward. Low-performance teams had far lower connectivity, asked almost no questions and showed almost no outward focus.

One of the most important things about Losada's observations is that the behaviour of the business teams reflected a complex system (called a *nonlinear dynamic system*). This is known commonly as the butterfly effect, in which seemingly trivial inputs can disproportionately determine later consequences elsewhere. It seems that positivity can produce disproportionate outcomes. The high-performance teams' behaviour was unpredictable and complex, with the focus of questions and language somewhat chaotic.

However, as Lucy Ryan (at Positive Insights) notes: 'the knock-on effect created lasting flexibility, creativity and above all, resilience when adversity hit'.

High-performance teams were not simply 'more and better' than low-performance teams. They had a collective synergy, and when other teams crumbled under pressure they bounced back with new questions and ideas. They were buoyed by their positivity ratio.

Something altogether different happened for the medium-performing teams. Following an encounter with extreme negativity, the 'butterfly' was not resilient – it got stuck in a rut – specifically at a point of negative, self-absorbed advocacy. That is, negativity caused the teams to lose their good cheer, their flexibility and their ability to question. They languished in an endless loop in which each person simply defended their own position and became critical of all else. They no longer listened to each other.

Interestingly, low-performance teams started where mixed-performance teams ended up. They were entrenched in self-absorbed advocacy – defending their own views and critical of all else. The dynamics showed that the teams spiralled down to a static point. This suggests that low-performance teams eventually lose flexibility altogether. They spiral down to a dead end – a stalemate.

So, in summary, the study demonstrated that with high-performance teams:

- Positivity went hand in hand with asking questions and focusing outwards.
- They were most open to new ideas.
- They operated in a synergistic way.
- Team members were more responsive to each other.
- Positivity was linked to business success.
- Positivity helped the team bounce back from adversity.
- They were more flexible and resilient.
- They never got stuck in critical, self-absorbed advocacy.

The tipping point

The positivity ratio of 3:1 – that is three positive emotions to each negative emotion – was identified as a precise tipping point (or 2.9301 if you really want precision!). That is, above this particular ratio the complex dynamics of flourishing emerge. Below this tipping point the cycles of languishing and failure lie.

More recent research (West *et al*, 2009) suggests that:

> *Team optimism is an important predictor of team outcomes when teams are newly formed, whereas team resilience and team efficacy show greater explanatory power after several team interactions.*

They go on to note that highly optimistic teams believe that they have control over their outcomes and success, which is a factor related to locus of control, and that individuals feel that they can make a difference.

How can you apply the research to your team?

In order to stand the best chance of developing a high-performing team, what follows is how you can apply the research. Firstly it can be useful to recognize your team's developmental stage (see Figure 11.1 on page 222). As the team goes through the forming stage you can facilitate introductions, but if it's a new team – however supportive and encouraging your words are – the next stage is storming. Here there's likely to be some testing of boundaries, whether the boundaries are around the scope of the project, ownerships of tasks or clarity of direction. To suppress conflict at this stage can push it underground and take longer to resolve, and therefore longer for the team to move into norming and ultimately performing. Without this awareness of the current stage, and what comes next, it would be too easy to think what you're doing isn't effective as opposed to seeing it as the necessary next stage to get to high performance.

If it's a new team, facilitating introductions can be the most effective step. If the team is currently in a storming stage, give space for individuals to work out their differences as it's often not effective for disagreements to go underground – far more effective for them to be resolved.

Whatever developmental stage the team is at, it seems that there are some universal 'things' that you can do: you can keep a tally and ensure you're making significantly more positive comments, you can ask more questions, you can direct the focus, and keep the team connected.

You can positively acknowledge comments and contributions from others, even when you disagree with the 'content' of what they're saying. For example, you can say things like 'that's an interesting perspective, thank you for adding it to our discussion'.

Ask questions to help clarify both your understanding, and their understanding: 'How do you see that working?' Ensure that the task and goal is clear – and that the required output is clear and understood by everyone.

The ability of the team to focus clearly on the task is important. In my experience this allows the expression of different viewpoints but all seeking to be resolved by focusing on the task at hand.

What's stopping you?

We've seen that there are specific traits and characteristics present in high-performing teams. These traits are available to each one of us – we can learn the skills to become more effective, and contribute to a more effective team.

Whilst it can be very easy to delay making any change until the leader changes his or her style, there are plenty of actions that you can take independently and these actions are likely to have a subtle influence on others. Of course you don't have to make these changes through stealth, not telling others of your intentions – you can be very overt in your suggestions to make a better working environment for yourself and the team, so that everyone can contribute and benefit.

Many organizations are looking for the next generation of leaders from amongst those who naturally begin to appear in team situations. I am not advocating rampant self-promotion or arrogance, which will get you noticed but not in an appropriate way. Rather, look for opportunities where you can take on extra responsibilities, or 'lead' a part of a project. Proactive behaviour that you deliver against will expand your experience, broaden your skills and add to your CV, while building your 'brand'.

In business, as in all our relationships, we must be able to navigate around obstacles. We achieve this through a number of social skills and a key skill is the one of negotiation which we shall look at next.

Summary

- Working in a highly effective team can be exhilarating as the team strives for, and achieves, more and more success – however, many teams do not reach this elusive state.
- Often we're not taught teamwork skills, and we do a good job of 'getting on with it' ... but there are teamwork skills that you can learn which are likely to increase your enjoyment of teamwork as well as massively increasing the team's effectiveness.
- The positivity ratio applies to learns.
- Understand the development stage of the team.

Note

1 I would like to give special thanks to Lucy Ryan at Positive Insights for her assistance with clarifying the original research, and her significant contribution to this section.

12
Negotiation

Whether you realize it or not, you're involved in negotiations on a daily basis. Even if you're not involved in 'proper' contractual negotiations, you are probably negotiating all the time whether with colleague, spouses, kids or friends, so before you skip this chapter, ponder on the quote from the film *Devil's Advocate*:

Protagonist: Are we negotiating?

Satan: Always.

In the same way we're often not given the tools to work in teams, often we're just not given the tools to negotiate. My experience suggests that most people use either logic or emotion when negotiating. Sometimes they use neither – blundering about – and rarely have awareness of both.

Two relevant skills to use in any business negotiations are the ability to research and find the pertinent facts, and be able to present them clearly and appropriately. However, this chapter is not about the 'content' of your negotiation, it is about the 'intangibles', sometimes known as emotional intelligence, which are equally important and possibly just as impactful as the first two elements. This chapter focuses more on some of the 'hard to nail' intangibles that can make the difference in your negotiations. Often just having 'sound logic' isn't enough, because people don't respond in what appears to be rational ways.

Under the banner of a field called 'behavioural economics' there is an experiment which clearly demonstrates the impact of lack of rationality.

A person is given $10 and is told that if they share the money with another person, who accepts, they can both keep the money. However, if the offer is rejected, neither party gets to keep the money. What would you offer? What would you accept?

Logic states that both are better off with 'some' rather than 'none' of the money, so any agreement is better than no agreement. Something that is surprising to many economists is that participants routinely offer about $4 of $10, and low offers of less than $2 are rejected half the time (Camerer, 1999).

You don't need me to tell you that people don't always respond in rational ways. However good an individual is at presenting the facts of a situation, there are additional skills that business negotiators can develop. These skills, in part, require the use of emotional awareness.

The following quote could be the description of a successful negotiator:

The ability to monitor one's own and others' feelings and emotions to discriminate among them, and to use this information to guide one's thinking and action.

It is, however, Salovey and Mayer's (1989) definition of emotional intelligence.

Practical tools

For many years the focus was on IQ – intelligence quotient as a predictor of success. There have been studies that show that IQ's not 'everything' and there are different types of intelligence which contribute to success. You may have heard about the importance of EQ – emotional quotient or emotional intelligence – to an individual's success. What follows are some practical things that you can do in order to develop your emotional awareness in negotiations. These are:

- managing one's own emotional state;
- structuring a conversation;
- understanding the other person's point of view;
- reinforcing patterns of behaviour;
- noticing others.

These are discussed below.

Managing one's emotional state

In a negotiation, often those of a personal nature, we become emotionally involved. Often we display our emotions, whether they're emotions of anger, frustration or joy. This is your emotional state. Sometimes these emotions can cloud our judgement and get in the way of negotiating. In business it's likely that you have on-going relationships with the people with whom you are negotiating, so it's useful to manage your emotional state. The OK Corral, described earlier in Chapter 10, is one tool that you can use.

Many people don't see themselves as regularly involved in negotiations on a daily basis. Subsequently the 'only' negotiations that they get involved in are of a more personal nature. For example, negotiating time off for holidays, or a salary increase. Personal topics can be very emotive.

As a manager, I've been on the receiving end of a full spectrum of emotions, and in my experience this emotional response doesn't do much to persuade me to change a decision that I've made.

Take a business negotiation which is about a high-value item. Up the stakes further, and on completion of this successful multi-million pound deal let's say that a percentage commission is payable to you, the negotiator. It can seem that others are trained to be rude, at least they can ask the 'difficult' questions – so not rising to their bait, and responding in a professional manner, is important.

When negotiating it's useful to be aware of your emotional state. I'm not suggesting you're devoid of emotion – just mindfully aware, and knowing how to become calmer. Mindful awareness (Chapter 5) is about noticing what's going on in the situation and remaining calm. Secondly use a skill that supports calmness, namely breathing. If you've ever noticed, when someone is panicky their breathing gets fast and shallow. Before a negotiation it can be useful to practise some HeartMath breathing (described in Chapter 9). During the meeting, pause occasionally to take a deeper breath. Deeper breathing will ensure that there's plenty of oxygen going to your brain, to enable you to think.

Structure of a conversation

Especially under stress, many people find themselves babbling, often incoherently. In negotiations, which are often stressful, this is more likely to happen. Therefore it can be useful to develop a structure to your everyday speech, so that in situations of higher stress you have a structure that you can depend on to hold you up.

'Structures' set the context for the conversation, present the facts and set clarity around the next actions suggested. There are different structures, but one I have used for many years is the 4MAT structure which is applicable in different contexts from training, presentations to business conversations.

The simplified version of the structure is 'Why, What, How and What-if'. The 'Why' describes the purpose, and why the other person should listen; the 'What' is relevant facts. The 'How' moves people to action, and the 'What-if' addresses any risks and objections. The beauty of this structure is its simplicity and accessibility, and no special skills are needed to use it, although the essential element is that you do use it.

EXAMPLE

<mini-what> What I'd like to discuss is the RFP. <why> The reason for this discussion is to make some immediate improvements to the report so that it can be delivered to the customer. <what> Specifically we need to add a section on post-implementation support. <how> Who do you think could contribute to that section? ... and <what if> if they're not around how will you get the section complete?

A second structure you may wish to consider is: framing, advocating, illustrating and inquiring. A conversation is 'framed' by setting the purpose. 'Advocating' is explicitly asserting an option or proposal for action. 'Illustrating' involves giving an example which 'puts meat on the bones' of the advocacy. 'Inquiring' involves asking others in order to learn something from them. This approach is described more fully in *Personal and Organisational Transformations Through Action Inquiry* (Fisher *et al*, 2000).

EXAMPLE

<framing> I'd like to make a recommendation for some new content on the website. <advocating> I'd like to recommend that we have short video clips. <illustrating> the way I see it we could have clips from each of the customer service representatives stating how we've helped other clients which would both add value and give a more personal look and feel to the website. <advocating> What do you think about this idea?

There are of course other approaches, but the above two are ones that I've used, and can recommend. It matters less as to which approach you use, just that you pick one and use it. More important is having *a* structure which provides you with a logical sequence to what you're saying. This enables your listener to more easily hear what you're saying, because they're not mentally darting around putting the pieces together.

Of course, however well you present the facts of the situation, however calm and professional you are, you're in conversation with another person who may well have a different perspective or point of view from your own. This has potential to produce a range of emotional responses depending on their level of EI. Here too you can employ the OK Corral while you manage your own energy and emotions.

Point of view

In any conversation there at least three perspectives: yours, the perspective of the other person, and a meta or detached perspective. With the different perspectives even facts can become ambiguous if not presented clearly.

First let's take a simplistic example of playing chess. Depending on which side of the table you're sitting at, the chess pieces will appear differently. As you look at the board the black king is on the left, and a white knight on the right. If you move and sit behind the table, the black king will appear on your right – and the white knight appears on the left. No wonder negotiations can become so protracted – just getting the facts clear can be challenging!

Now imagine you are negotiating an outsourcing contract which represents many millions of euros and will affect the jobs of whole departments. If you are representing union members your perspective will be one of trying to protect your members, if you are the employer then you want to reduce costs and streamline the organization to increase profitability and hopefully competitiveness. If you are representing the outsourcer (the company that will take over the old employees and sell the services back to the company) you will be concerned about costs and limiting the unknown.

Each party has its own perspective and strong reasons to act in a given way to see a desired outcome. Add to this negotiations where

FIGURE 12.1   A matter of perspective

someone doesn't have the relevant facts or intentionally or unintentionally obscures them. It's easy to see this as a negotiation, and often there are staff who specialize in this type of negotiation. However, we're involved in negotiations at work all the time. When to complete a piece of work? What goes in the report? Who to involve in a meeting? ... these all offer potential for negotiation even if we don't think of ourselves as negotiators.

When going into negotiations, I find it useful to remember that I may not see the full picture, or the picture I'm seeing may be biased. This enables me to ask questions to clarify whether something is from my perspective or more pervasive.

Reinforcing patterns of behaviour

In my experience, we often see the other party as the 'difficult' one in the conversation or negotiation. Sometimes we just don't see how what we're doing is contributing to the other person being 'difficult'.

When we're 'in' the system it can be especially difficult to get the meta view so that we can see how we're perpetuating the 'system'. Here is a short example, which while quite old amply illustrates the point. In 1997, on *BBC Newsnight* interviewer Jeremy Paxman asked the same question to his interviewee – 'Did you threaten to overrule him?' – a total of 12 times in succession.

Why was the question asked again and again? Because the interviewee didn't clearly answer yes or no – but came back with 'his position', and lots of other information other than a 'yes' or 'no'!

If you ever find you are continually being asked the same (awkward) question, consider the possibility that it might be because you're not answering the question!

Developing your self-awareness enables you to notice when you're likely to be perpetuating negative and reinforcing patterns of behaviour. The next skill is honing your awareness of other people.

Noticing others

Perhaps in the highest echelons negotiators have poker faces and don't give any 'tells' in their negotiations. However in my experience people are generally themselves, and they give us plenty of clues, both verbal and non-verbal, as to how they're reacting to what's been said.

Some people have a more physically telling emotional response than others. Calibration is more than just using a dictionary of body language to broadly categorize the response, it is the deliberate act of noticing what forms an individual's verbal and non-verbal cues. For example, when some people agree, they may do it with gusto and full-blown enthusiasm. For others agreement might be understated and slight. If you're expecting a full-blown enthusiastic agreement, but you're negotiating with someone who is less enthusiastic, you may reach agreement without even realizing it.

Notice the moment-by-moment changes in someone's body language. With this 'other awareness' a negotiator might (internally) question what's prompted the change, or notice whether the other party is broadly in agreement or disagreement with what's being said. It can be absolutely central to the success of the negotiation, as it can influence your timing, help you to notice that more information is needed, prompt you to listen more, or to restate the objectives and the goal to keep focus.

Of course the more people involved in a negotiation, the harder this is, but start with one person, and start in a non-critical negotiation. These skills don't come overnight, they require practice.

What does the research say?

The skills required in negotiation are the skills of emotional intelligence. They can be practised in your everyday dealings with people. My suggestion is to start with small interactions in the relatively safe environment of work, or with friends and family, before trying out significant business negotiations.

The Mayer-Salovey-Caruso Emotional Intelligence Test (MSCEIT™) was developed by academics at Yale and the University of New Hampshire. The scale evaluates EI through a series of objective and impersonal questions. It tests the respondent's ability to perceive, use, understand and regulate emotions. Typically, the first stage of awareness is to increase our awareness of our emotions before developing the skills of noticing the other person. You might begin to notice their facial expressions, and changes in posture. How tuned in are you to the overall mood of the situation? You already know how to lighten a mood, or to make encouraging comments to facilitate the receptivity of ideas. Another skill to develop is the skill of timing. In the same way you wouldn't ask your new employer for a pay rise on the first day of the job, there is skill in knowing 'when' to ask a more challenging question.

Whether your role requires significant negotiation or teamwork, this book has provided you with tools to work with your team in a more supportive manner, and not be caught out by poor communication.

This increases the likelihood that you will be part of a high-performing team – with the inherent reward of the team buzz and the fulfilling spiral of achievement. The book has provided tools to manage your emotions, to put in place practices that enable you to become more efficient and perhaps find time and opportunity to savour at work. Wherever your journey to achieving great days at work started from, you will have the tools to increase your levels of positive emotions and therefore maximize your opportunities for personal and professional success.

Summary

- Typically our days at work are filled with negotiations even if we don't think of ourselves as negotiators.

- Negotiations are the art and science of two or more people reaching a decision.

- Decisions often involve elements of emotion; this is often forgotten when we negotiate.

- There is a place for logic and emotion in negotiations; these are two very different sets of skills, and most of us typically don't have both naturally. However, both can be learned.

- Logic includes the ability to present the relevant facts clearly and appropriately.

- However well you present facts clearly, people don't always seem to respond in a logical way.

- It's useful therefore to develop skills of emotional awareness and emotional management.

- Skills include: managing one's emotional state; having a structure for moments of high stress; the ability to see things from different points of view; recognizing when we contribute to a problem; and observing others.

References

Allen, D D (2001) *Getting Things Done: How to achieve stress-free productivity*, Piatkus, London

Ariely, D (2008) *Predictably Irrational: The hidden forces that shape our decisions*, HarperCollins, New York

Babyak, M *et al* (2000) Exercise treatment for major depression: Maintenance of therapeutic benefit at 10 months, *Psychosomatic Medicine*, 62, pp 633–38

Back, K and Back, K (1999) *Assertiveness at Work: A practical guide to handling awkward situations*, McGraw-Hill, London

Baumeister, R F *et al* (2003) Does high self-esteem cause better performance, interpersonal success, happiness, or healthier lifestyles?, *Psychological Science in the Public Interest*, 4, pp 1–44

Beck, D and Cowan, C C (2006) *Spiral Dynamics: Mastering values, leadership and change: explaining the new science of memetics*, Blackwell, Oxford

Berne, E (1971) *A Layman's Guide to Psychiatry and Psychoanalysis*, Penguin, Harmondsworth

Biddle, J H and Mutrie, N (2001) *Psychology of Physical Activity: Determinants, well-being and interventions*, Routledge, New York

Boniwell, I *et al* (2010) A question of balance: Time perspective and well-being in British and Russian samples, *The Journal of Positive Psychology*, 5, pp 24–40

Buckingham, M and Coffman, C (2005) *First, Break All the Rules: what the world's greatest managers do differently*, Pocket, London

Camerer, C (1999) Behavioural economics: reunifying psychology and economics, *Proceedings of the National Academy of Sciences*, 96, pp 10575–77

Chabris, C F and Simons, D J (2010) *The Invisible Gorilla: And other ways our intuitions deceive us*, Crown, New York

Charlesworth, A (2013) Entrepreneurs Succeed with US, Troubador Publishing (in press)

Cheng, C (2003) Cognitive and motivational processes underlying coping flexibility: A dual-process model, *Journal of Personality and Social Psychology*, **84**, pp 425–38

Collins, J C (2001) *Good to Great: Why some companies make the leap – and others don't*, Random House Business, London

Cook-Greuter, S R (2004) Making the case for a developmental perspective, *Industrial and Commercial Training*, **36**, pp 275–81

Covey, S R (1989) *The Seven Habits of Highly Effective People: Restoring the character ethic*, Simon and Schuster, London

Coyle, D (2009) *The Talent Code: Unlocking the secret of skill in maths, art, music, sport, and just about everything else*, Random House, London

Csikszentmihalyic, M (2002) *Flow: The classic work on how to achieve happiness*, Rider, London

Davidson, R J and Lutz, A (2008) Buddha's brain: Neuroplasticity and meditation [In the Spotlight], *Signal Processing Magazine*, **25**, pp 176–74

De Bono, E (2000) *Six Thinking Hats*, Penguin, London

Dement, W C and Vaughan, C C (2000) *The Promise of Sleep: The scientific connection between health, happiness, and a good night's sleep*, Macmillan, London

Dweck, C S (2006) *Mindset: The new psychology of success*, Random House, New York

Ernst, F (1971) The OK Corral: The grid for get-on-with. *Transactional Analysis Journal*, **1**, pp 231–40

Espen, R (2006) *The Science of Well-being* (eds F Huppert, N Baylis and B Keverne), Oxford University Press, New York

Fave, A D and Massimini, F (2005) The investigation of optimal experience and apathy: Developmental and psychosocial implications, *European Psychologist*, **10**, pp 264–74

Feltz, D L and Landers, D M (1983) The effects of mental practice on motor skill learning and performance: A meta-analysis. *Journal of Sport Psychology*, **5**, pp 25–57

Felzt, D L and Landers, D M (2007) The effects of mental practice on motor skill learning and performance: A meta-analysis. In: Smith, D and Bar-Eli, M (eds) *Essential Readings in Sport and Exercise Psychology*, Champaign, IL, Human Kinetics

Fisher, D, Rooke, D & Torbert, W R (2003) *Personal and Organisational Transformations: Through action enquiry*, Edge/Work Press

Fowler, J H and Christakis, N A (2009) Dynamic spread of happiness in a large social network: Longitudinal analysis over 20 years in the Framingham Heart Study, *British Medical Journal*, 338, pp 1–13

Frankl, V E (2004) *Man's Search for Meaning: The classic tribute to hope from the Holocaust*, Rider, London

Fredrickson, B L (2001) The role of positive emotions in positive psychology: The broaden-and-build theory of positive emotions, *American Psychologist*, 56, pp 218–26

Fredrickson, B L (2009) *Positivity: Groundbreaking research reveals how to embrace the hidden strength of positive emotions, overcome negativity, and thrive*, Crown Publishers, New York

Fredrickson, B L and Losada, M F (2005) Positive affect and the complex dynamics of human flourishing, *American Psychologist*, 60, pp 678–86

Froh, J J et al (2007) Interpersonal relationships and irrationality as predictors of life satisfaction, *Journal of Positive Psychology*, 2, pp 29–39

Gable, S L, Reiss, H T, Impelt, E A and Asher, E R (2004) What do you do when things go right? The intrapersonal and interpersonal benefits of sharing positive events, *Journal of Personality and Social Psychology*, 87, pp 228–45

Gallwey, W T (1986) *The Inner Game of Golf*, Pan, London

Gilbert, D (2002) Decisions and revisions: The affective forecasting of changeable outcomes, *Journal of Personality and Social Psychology*, 82, pp 503–14

Gilbert, D (2004) *Why are we happy? Why aren't we happy?* [Online]. TED. Available: http://www.youtube.com/watch?v=LTO_dZUvbJA [Accessed 26 July 2011]

Godin, S (2007) *The Dip: The extraordinary benefits of knowing when to quit (and when to stick)*, Piatkus, London

Graham, S M et al (2008) The positives of negative emotions: willingness to express negative emotions promotes relationships, *Personality & Social Psychology Bulletin*, 34, pp 394–406

Grant, A (2006) An integrative goal-focused approach to executive coaching. In Stober, D R and Grant, A M (eds) *Evidence Based Coaching Handbook: Putting best practices to work for your clients*, John Wiley and Sons Inc, Hoboken, NJ

Gregory, W L, Cialdini, R B and Carpenter, K M (1982) Self-relevant scenarios as mediators of likelihood estimates and compliance: Does imagining make it so?, *Journal of Personality and Social Psychology*, 43, pp 89–99

Hazelton, S (2012) *Raise Your Game: How to build on your successes to achieve transformational results*, Ecademy Press

Hiroto, D S and Seligman, M E (1975) Generality of learned helplessness in man, *Journal of Personality and Social Psychology*, **31**, pp 311–27

Hood, B (2012) *The Self Illusion*, Constable and Robinson Ltd, UK

Huppert, F A (2009) Psychological Well-being: Evidence Regarding its Causes and Consequences. *Applied Psychology: Health and Well-Being*, (2), pp 137–64

Isen, A M (2009) A role for neuropsychology in understanding the facilitating influence of positive affect on social behavior and cognitive processes. In Lopez, S J and Snyder, C R (eds) *Oxford Handbook of Positive Psychology*, Oxford University Press, New York

Kahneman, D (2012) *Thinking fast and slow*, Penguin, London

Kappes, H B and Oettingen, G (2011) Positive fantasies about idealized futures sap energy, *Journal of Experimental Social Psychology*, **47**, pp 719–29

Karpmen, S (1968) Fairy tales and script drama analysis, *Transactional Analysis Bulletin*, **7**, pp 39–43

Kashdan, T B and Rottenberg, J (2010) Psychological flexibility as a fundamental aspect of health, *Clinical Psychology Review*, **30**, pp 467–80

King, L A and Miner, K N (2000) Writing about the perceived benefits of traumatic events: implications for physical health, *Personality and Social Psychology Bulletin*, **26**, pp 220–30

King, L A, Scollon, C K, Ramsey, C and Williams, T (2000) Stories of life transition: Subjective well-being and ego development in parents of children with Down Syndrome, *Journal of Research in Personality*, **34**, pp 509–36

Kiyosaki, R T, Lechter, S L and Kiyosaki, R T (1999) *Rich Dad's Cashflow euadrant: Employee, self-employed, business owner, or investor... which is the best quadrant for you?*, New York, Warner Business; Maidenhead, Melia [distributor]

Kofodimos, J R (1990) Why executives lose their balance, *Organizational Dynamics*, **19**, pp 58–73

Langer, E J and Rodin, J (1976) The effects of choice and enhanced personal responsibility for the aged: A field experiment in an institutional setting, *Journal of Personality and Social Psychology*, **34**, pp 191–98

Law, S (2007) *Philosophy*, Dorling Kindersley, London

Lazarus, R S and Folkman, S (1987) Transactional theory and research on emotions and coping, *European Journal of Personality*, **1**, pp 141–69

Linley, P A and Joseph, S (eds) (2004) *Positive Psychology in Practice,* Wiley, Hoboken, NJ

Loehr, J E and Schwartz, T (2003) *The Power of Full Engagement: Managing energy, not time, is the key to high performance and personal renewal,* Free Press, New York

Loftus, E F and Palmer, J C (1974) Reconstruction of automobile destruction: An example of the interaction between language and memory, *Journal of Verbal Learning and Verbal Behavior,* **13**, pp 585–89

Loftus, E F and Palmer, J C (1996) Reconstruction of automobile destruction: An example of the interaction between language and memory. In Fein, S and Spencer, S (eds) *Readings in Social Psychology: The art and science of research,* Houghton, Mifflin and Company, Boston, MA

Lopez, S J *et al* (2004) Strategies for Accentuating Hope. In Linley, P A and Joseph, S (eds) *Positive Psychology in Practice,* John Wiley and Sons Inc, Hoboken, NJ

Lyubomirsky, S (2010) *The How of Happiness: A practical approach to getting the life you want,* Piatkus, London

Marmot, M G and Smith, G D (1991) Health inequalities among British civil servants: The Whitehall II study, *Lancet,* **337**, p 1387

McAdams, D P (1992) Unity and purpose in human lives: The emergence of identity as a life story. In Zucker, R A, Rabin, A I, Aronoff, J and Frank, S J (eds) *Personality Structure in the Life Course: Essays on personology in the Murray tradition,* Springer Publishing Co, New York.

McCarthy, B and O'Neill-Blackwell, J (2007) *Hold On, You Lost Me!: Use learning styles to create training that sticks,* ASTD Press, Alexandria, Va

McDonald, T and Langer, E (2010) *The Young Ones* [Online]. BBC. [Accessed 27 April 2011].

McGregor, I and Little, B R (1998) Personal projects, happiness, and meaning: On doing well and being yourself, *Journal of Personality and Social Psychology,* **74**, pp 494–512

Meichenbaum, D (2009) Stress inoculation training. In O'Donohue, W T and Fisher, J E (eds) *General Principles and Empirically Supported Techniques of Cognitive Behavior Therapy,* John Wiley and Sons Inc, Hoboken, NJ

Moiso, C (1984) *TA: The State of the Art,* Foris Publications, Dordrecht

Neenan, M and Dryden, W (2002) *Life Coaching: A cognitive-behavioural approach,* Brunner-Routledge, Hove

Nolen-Hoeksema, S (2003) *Women Who Think Too Much: How to break free of overthinking and reclaim your life*, Piatkus, London

Olds, J and Milner, P (1954) Positive Reinforcement Produced by Electrical Stimulationof Septal Area and Other Regions of Rat Brain. *Journal of Comparative and Physiological Psychology*, **47**, pp 419–27

Peterson, C F (2006) *A Primer in Positive Psychology*, Oxford University Press, New York

Pink, D (2009) *Drive: The surprising truth about what motivates us*, Riverhead Books, New York

Rath, T and Clifton, D O (2005) *How Full is Your Bucket? Positive strategies for work and life*, Gallup, New York

Reivich, K and Shatté, A (2002) *The Resilience Factor: 7 essential skills for overcoming life's inevitable obstacles*, Broadway Books, New York

Roepke, S K and Grant, I (2011) Toward a more complete understanding of the effects of personal mastery on cardiometabolic health, *Health Psychology*, **30**, pp 615–32

Rogers, L and Angelini, F (2011) Life begins at 90, *The Sunday Times*, 24 April, p 6

Rohn, E J (1985) *7 Strategies for Wealth and Happiness: Power ideas from America's foremost business philosopher*, Prima, Roseville, CA [Great Britain]

Rooke, D and Torbert, W R (2005) Seven Transformations of Leadership, *Harvard Business Review*

Rowe, D (1988) *The Successful Self*, Fontana, London

Ryan, R M and Deci, E L (2000) Self-determination theory and the facilitation of intrinsic motivation, social development, and well-being, *American Psychologist*, **55**, pp 68–78

Salovey, P and Mayer, J D (1989) Emotional Intelligence, *Imagination, Cognition and Personality*, **9**, pp 185–211

Schwartz, B (2004) *The Paradox of Choice: Why more is less*, ECCO, New York

Schwartz, S (2005) *Basic Human Values: An overview*, The Hebrew University of Jerusalem, Jerusalem

Schwartz, T, Gomes, J and McCarthy, C (2010) *The Way We're Working Isn't Working: The four forgotten needs that energize great performance*, Simon and Schuster, London

Sedlmeier, P, Eberth, J, Schwarz, M, Zimmerman, D, Haarig, F, Jaeger, S and Kunze, S (2012) The psychological effects of meditation: a meta-analysis, *Psychological Bulletin*

Seligman, M E P *et al* (2005) Positive psychology progress: empirical validation of interventions, *American Psychologist*, **60**, pp 410–21

Shapiro, S L, Schwartz, G E R and Santerre, C (2009) Meditation and positive psychology. In Lopez, S J and Snyder, C R (eds) *Oxford Handbook of Positive Psychology*, Oxford University Press, New York

Stanovich, K E (2010) *How to Think Straight About Psychology*, Pearson, Boston

Steger, M F and Frazier, P (2005) Meaning in life: one link in the chain from religiousness to well-being, *Journal of Counseling Psychology*, **52**, pp 574–82

Stewart, I and Joines, V (1987) *TA Today: A new introduction to transactional analysis*, Lifespace, Nottingham

Strack, F, Martin, L L and Stepper, S (1988) Inhibiting and facilitating conditions of the human smile: A nonobtrusive test of the facial feedback hypothesis, *Journal of Personality and Social Psychology*, **54**, pp 768–77

Suttie, J (2006) *Your perfect swing*, Champaign, IL; Human Kinetics, Leeds

Tapscott, D and Williams, A D (2008) *Wikinomics: How mass collaboration changes everything*, Atlantic, London

Taylor, S E *et al* (1998) Harnessing the imagination: Mental simulation, self-regulation, and coping, *American Psychologist*, **53**, pp 429–39

Tennen, H and Affleck, G (2002) Benefit-finding and benefit-reminding. In Snyder, C R and Lopez, S J (eds) *Handbook of Positive Psychology*, Oxford University Press, New York

Tuckman, B W (1965) Developmental sequence in small groups, *Psychological Bulletin*, **63**, pp 384–99

Ulrich, D and Ulrich, W (2010) *The Why of Work: How great leaders build abundant organizations that win*, McGraw-Hill, Maidenhead

Verme, P (2009) Happiness, freedom and control, *Journal of Economic Behavior & Organization*, **71**, pp 146–61

Wansink, B, Painter, J E and Lee, Y K (2006) The office candy dish: proximity's influence on estimated and actual consumption, *International Journal of Obesity*, **30**, pp 871–75

West, B J, Patera, J L and Carsten, M K (2009) Team level positivity: Investigating positive psychological capacities and team level outcomes, *Journal of Organizational Behavior*, **30**, pp 249–67

Wiseman, R (2003) The Luck Factor, *Skeptical Inquirer*, May/June edn

Zimbardo, P G and Boyd, J (2008) *The Time Paradox: The new psychology of time*, Rider, London

Index